Caroline Franczia

POPCORN
FOR THE NEW
CEO
Vol. II

Snackable content from meetings and
missions with Fortune 500, Venture
Capitalists and Scale-ups executives

'We delight in the beauty of the butterfly, but rarely admit the changes it has gone through to achieve that beauty.'

Maya Angelou

DEDICATION

To Capucine, Charlotte, Garance,

you are the women of tomorrow.

To Romeo & Theodore,

you remain my biggest inspiration, every day.

FOREWORD BY ANDY WHYTE

Caroline and I met in 2015 at rapid growth Unicorn, Sprinklr, back when Unicorns were as rare as... well, Unicorns.

It was immediately apparent Caroline had that je ne sais quoi. The rarely talked about attribute of top salespeople who can capture and hold the attention of top execs. This ability to connect and become a trusted advisor takes more than what many laud as confidence. Confidence is merely the impression you give that lays upon the abundance of skills you need to operate effectively at the top table.

Skills such as leadership, strategic thinking, adaptability, problem-solving, and the ability to build relationships with all stakeholders.

These skills are the hallmarks of the modern CEO, whose role has never been more challenging. Having to navigate the complexities of corporate objectives and building diverse teams while utilizing modern tools, frameworks, and strategies to ensure their organizations meet their potential. They have their work cut out for themselves.

CEOs cannot look to their teams for the answers to these things. They are supposed to have the solutions, and, with the frugality of a CEO's time, the role can appear isolated.

This is the reason why Caroline's sequel to her incredible first book (Popcorn for the new CEO) is so wildly brilliant.

This book artfully combines the worlds of sales and leadership, demonstrating the interconnectedness between the two and the value of a sales-oriented mindset for a CEO while doing so in a sharp, clear, and to-the-point manner (with just the right amount of links to movies as anyone could want).

One of the key strengths of this book lies in its practical approach, offering actionable advice and real-life examples that will resonate with readers. Caroline's emphasis on building effective operations, managing modern workforces, and Go-To-Market strategies that crush will prove invaluable for new CEOs seeking to establish a strong foundation for their leadership journey.

As you delve into the pages of this book, you will discover the parallels between successful revenue leaders and effective CEOs and learn how to harness these shared qualities to propel your organization toward success. This book is a treasure trove of knowledge and a testament to Caroline's passion for helping businesses grow and thrive.

Whether you are a new CEO or an aspiring leader, this book will undoubtedly serve as an invaluable resource as you navigate the exciting and challenging world of business leadership.

From this point on, you are going to need a few things:
1. A highlighter.
2. A comfortable chair.
3. Plenty of spare time, as you are not going to be able to put this book down.

Enjoy, and May your Champions be Strong

Andy Whyte

Andy Whyte is the Chief Executing Officer and Founder of MEDDICC™, he is passionate about the science and art of sales. Author of the five-star rated "MEDDICC' book, one of his famous quote is "Nobody ever regrets qualifying out". Andy is passionate about the science and art of sales.

FOREWORD BY JEN ALLEN KNUTH

A seasoned expert in complex selling, Jen Allen Knuth enlights us with sharp linkedin post useful for all sales, even the most successful ones. Jen met the author while recording an episode of the podcast she used to be the host of in her role as the Chief Evangelist Officer for Challenger sales, a methodology Caroline enjoys referring to and rely upon. During the interview, Jen took the opportunity to explore Caroline's perspective of negotiations through the voice and perspective of Jack Sparrow, a chapter of Popcorn for the new CEO.

'Caroline has an impeccable way of making business advice snackable, entertaining, and memorable. Popcorn for the New CEO 2 leaves no stone unturned, all while delighting the reader with practical call to actions that will help any CEO or founder see around corners. This is a must-read!'

BOOK I:

CORPORATE PERSPECTIVE

CORPORATE OBJECTIVES

Cool runnings[1]

They lived on an island with an average temperature of 30°C. They had no training gear, no experience, and no coach. Yet, they fixed an impossible goal: join the 1988 Winter Olympics in Calgary. Whether the actual story or the movie inspires you, Cool Runnings will help you set the tone for your fiscal year and hopefully make it a peaceful journey.

Yul: 'Very strong.'

---

[1] Photo credit: Pixabay

Coach Irv: 'Nice, very nice, but... what exactly does it mean?'

Derice: 'Cool runnings means, 'peace be the journey.'

When setting goals, the leanest and most effective way to begin is with a single document called a 'value pyramid.' To help align your team members' expectations, you'll need: a one-pager that defines your company objective, business strategies, supporting initiatives and required capabilities to achieve them in simple bullet points.

Irwin Blitzer: 'Whether you win or lose a bobsleigh race, it's all about right here, the push-start! And this is where you're gonna learn about the push- start, right here in a Volkswagen!'

The value pyramid[2] starts with the company goal, aka your corporate objective. It should be simple and measurable. In large corporations, the corporate objective is usually laid out clearly in the 10K or annual report.

---

[2] At the end of this chapter you will find an example of how to create a Value pyramid for your prospect, it can be used for prospecting, account planning and customer success management

Examples are: achieve 5% growth by {date}, or grab 12% marketshare by {date}. It aligns with either increasing revenue, decreasing cost, or reducing risk. In the startup world, the most generic corporate objective is to achieve a certain revenue level or achieve profitability.

Irwin Blitzer: 'Gentlemen, a bobsled is a simple thing.'

The corporate objective should be known, shared, and owned by all departments. It represents the true north to all employees since everyone should positively impact the company's corporate goal.

To achieve the company goal, startup and scaleup executives will define a set of business strategies aligned with customer satisfaction. Remember that acquisition is worth nothing if you have a high churn rate[3].

The business strategies will often attach to the following categories: operational excellence, talent, product, marketing, and client-facing. Examples of business strategies are: open new offices and expand internationally, add new revenue streams to your

---

[3] Popcorn for the new CEO, 2021. Chap 18: 0% churn rate

catalog, transform your client-facing team towards complex selling (large deals with large accounts), etc.

The key here is to stay true to your roots and your vision.

Sanka Coffie: 'I'm freezing my royal Rastafarian na-nas off!'

VCs, advisors, and other successful scaleups will influence your path, but this is the time to own what your company is about and define an approach that works for your business.

Sanka Coffie: 'All I'm saying, mon, is if we walk Jamaican, talk Jamaican, and is Jamaican, then we sure as hell better bobsleg Jamaican.'

Egos should remain at the door. A team does not work without execution. And execution does not work without a set of clearly defined roles and responsibilities. To determine your business strategies, you must own all available data from the field –customer product feedback, sales difficulties, marketing alignment – and measure it.

Sanka Coffie:'You don't understand, I am Sanka Coffie, I am the best pushcart driver in all of Jamaica! I must drive! Do you dig where I'm coming from?'

Irv: 'Yeah, I dig where you're coming from.'

Sanka Coffie: 'Good.'

Irv: 'Now dig where I'm coming from. I'm coming from two gold medals. I'm coming from nine world records in both the two- and four-man events. I'm coming from ten years of intense competition with the best athletes in the world.'

Sanka Coffie: 'That's a hell of a place to be coming from!'

Heads of departments – such as the CPO, CRO, and CMO – will develop several initiatives to support the business strategies. The initiatives are often translated into OKRs with their team. It is crucial that each individual, no matter their level, knows how their OKRs impact the company's success.

Yul Brenner: 'You see Junior? Well, let me tell you what I see. I see pride! I see power! I see a bad-ass mother who don't take no crap off of nobody!'

Execution is key. Lean implementation is even better:

- Ensure that all internal meetings are the right length of time and have a clear, shared agenda, objectives and follow ups.

- If these meetings only need to happen bi-weekly, do not saturate the calendar by making them weekly.

- Cross-departmental synchronization is essential. Ensure that your teams monitor all KPIs on a weekly/ monthly and quarterly basis. You cannot make decisions if you do not have the data.

Sanka Coffie: 'Feel the rhythm! Feel the rhyme! get on up because it's bobsleg time, Cool Runnings!'

Finally, your company value pyramid should be accessible to everyone in the organization, easy to read, easy to digest, and updated as much as external factors

(Pandemix, War, Economics..) and adaptability[4] require it.

Doing so will enable the entire company to get into an operating rhythm, allowing employees to achieve their personal goals while constantly attaching to the company objectives at the same time – by working with other teams towards a common goal.

Sanka Coffie: 'I am feeling very Olympic today, how about you?'

---

[4] Popcorn for the new CEO, 2023. Chap 4: Entrepreneurs & Adaptability quotient

<u>Plot summary</u>

- ❖ Your company should align on a true north: your corporate objectives.
- ❖ To achieve the ultimate goal you must have clear, shared business strategies.
- ❖ Each department will attach and support these strategies with initiatives.
- ❖ To adjust your actions and their value, make sure to measure them with KPIs.
- ❖ Don't forget that cross departmental synchronisation is essential.

<u>Ready, set, action!</u>

- ❖ What is your company goal? Have you shared it with everyone? Can anyone attach to the true north? How do you communicate about it? How often?
- ❖ How do you ensure cross departments alignment and synchronization? Do all initiatives of each department attach to the same business strategies? Corporate goal?

Corporate Objective	[Add a Corporate Objective here that can be translated into financial goals and we can attach our value proposition to. Add a link or a comment about your source.]		
Business Strategy	[Add the Business Strategy #1 supporting the above mentioned objective. Add a link or a comment about your source.]	[Add the Business Strategy #1 supporting the above mentioned objective. Add a link or a comment about your source.]	[Add the Business Strategy #1 supporting the above mentioned objective. Add a link or a comment about your source.]
Business Initiatives	[Add 3-5 Business Initiatives here supporting the above mentioned strategy. Add a link or a comment about your source.]	[Add 3-5 Business Initiatives here supporting the above mentioned strategy. Add a link or a comment about your source.]	[Add 3-5 Business Initiatives here supporting the above mentioned strategy. Add a link or a comment about your source.]
Required Capabilities	[Add the Required Capabilities necessary to achieve the above mentioned business initiatives]	[Add the Required Capabilities necessary to achieve the above mentioned business initiatives]	[Add the Required Capabilities necessary to achieve the above mentioned business initiatives]
Proof Points	Add a sentence from a Customer Story here that is relevant to the above. Add a link to the story if possible.	Add a sentence from a Customer Story here that is relevant to the above. Add a link to the story if possible.	Add a sentence from a Customer Story here that is relevant to the above. Add a link to the story if possible.

ASSESSING PROBLEM-MARKET FIT

The x Files [5]

A founder has a great idea, a start-up develops a great product, but how do you know if there is an actual market for it? How do you know how to be product-disruptive (or service-disruptive) and generate revenue simultaneously?

To many, solving this case can be as mystic and troublesome as the Federal Bureau of Investigation agents Dana Scully and Fox Mulder's X-files.

[5] **Photo by** Stephen Leonardi **on** Unsplash

Agent Dana Scully: 'The truth is out there, but so are lies.'

The Problem-Market fit is not only creating a solution through a product or a service to a problem; it is also the level at which that solution satisfies strong market demand.

The biggest mistake a start-up can make in its beginning is to focus on winning customers that are not aligned with their vision for the sake of "winning" customers. Opportunistic revenue might be some money in the bank, yet, it can also be damaging in the long run. Opportunistic revenue can have an impact on future sales and their price per value, as much as weight on resources, and in some cases deviation of the roadmap and your vision to serve customers who...well, never bought your vision. When you sign a customer, and it comes to you through the network, you hardly have to understand their problems. In many of these cases, it was an easy and fast signature: you were too cheap, you did not prove your value, you stayed in your comfort zone.

Special Agent Dana Scully: 'I have to be in Washington, D.C. in 11 hours for a hearing, the outcome of which might affect one of the biggest decisions of my life, and here I am in the middle of nowhere, Texas, chasing phantom tanker trucks.'

Don't run the pity show with the most common excuse of all 'but people don't know they need me yet. I am disrupting the industry'. Many start-ups, which then became scaleup and successful public companies, overcame this matter, so will you. You've got this.

Agent Dana Scully: 'Any thoughts as to why anybody would be growing corn in the middle of the desert?'

Yes, it is possible to sell where there was no budget line. Yes, you can sell even though your prospect does not know he/she needs your product.
Yes, it is possible to sell at a high value.

But only if you bring value to the table. Your product may sell itself if it is the self-service type (PLG). But it is fixing an issue for the community that is picking up on it.

Special Agent Dana Scully: 'Please explain to me the scientific nature of the whammy.'

A company that looks into fixing a problem, usually a technical or functional problem such as "I cannot do something" will want to write their RFP and do their own research before meeting you.

If you push only benefits, expect your prospects to buy a nice-to-have solution, therefore at a low value.

It is, therefore, your responsibility to make your prospect verbalize their functional problems, make them share with you what they cannot do.

Your value proposition lies in how you can fix this particular functional/operation problem better than anyone else with an impact on their business.

But be careful, operational issues in themselves do not carry a significant budget associated with it if it does not impact a) revenue, b) cost, and/or c) reputation.

Assistant Director Walter Skinner (to Agent Fox Mulder): 'You and I both know that if it looks bad, it's bad for the FBI. Blame has to be assigned somewhere.'

Sometimes, you simply cannot have this type of conversation because the prospect will not allow it, because of an official RFP, it is better to qualify out gently.

Your chances of winning are slim.

Every time I did so, I protected my team, and occasionally enough, we won by changing the prospect mindset.

We were able to turn the tables around by walking away with respect: "We understand your current situation, we believe we can bring a lot to the table because of the expertise we have developed. Nevertheless, the setup you wish for us to respond to is not in line with our long-term vision for our customers. Therefore, we will not respond to the RFP as it is written. We are, however, more than happy to share our vision of the future, a disruptive manner of fixing your issue through an open workshop".

Special Agent Dana Scully: 'I don't have time for your convenient ignorance.'

To ensure that you get the most valuable conversations with prospects, make sure to choose your early adopters, the right companies at the right time. For this, do not stop at the type of market you can address, such as large companies vs mid-market. Instead, try to understand your personas. Who are you targeting? How do they work? What is their process? What are their struggles? Are you in alignment with their vision? What have you identified they cannot do, and you can solve?

Last but not least, your problem-market fit does not lie in some kind of return on investment (ROI) that you cannot guarantee. For over twenty years, suppliers have pushed the idea that their solution can bring hard (dollars) and soft ROIs. News flash: your buyers are aware that in 90% of cases, it is bullshit. You cannot manage the resources they will allocate, the processes they will put in position, nor adoption.

ROI is in fact, quite fictitious in most cases. Nonetheless, you define a set of meaningful KPIs to watch and improve. This is how your company will be sticky: by providing real value and building trust.

Agent Fox Mulder: 'Trust no one."And that's hard, Scully. Suspecting everyone, everything, it wears you down. You even begin to doubt what you know is the truth.''

Plot summary
- ❖ You must align your product with the value you can bring to the table.
- ❖ If you disrupt an industry you must educate your prospect and win the market you have identified.
- ❖ Finding your early adopters is essential to your thriving and scaling

---

Ready, set, action!
- ❖ Have you ever been in the situation when you had to qualify out a prospect that would consume too much of your resources? Were you able to do it?

GO TO MARKET STRATEGIES

Harry Potter

Hufflepuff, Gryffindor, or Ravenclaw: which revenue generation house are you? There are many ways of identifying and determining which revenue architecture or which sales path is right for your solution and your company. In Harry Potter, both the books and the movies, the Sorting Hat has a significant impact on the course of Hogward's students. Depending on where the

Storting Hat places them, their entire development and learning journey will defer.

> *'The founders put some brains in me*
> *So I could choose instead!*
> *Now slip me snug around your ears,*
> *I've never yet been wrong,*
> *I'll have a look inside your mind*
> *And tell you where you belong!'*
> — *The Sorting Hat*

Luckily, unlike at Hogwarts, in the startup and scaleup life, if you believe you've taken the wrong track, you may change houses smoothly. There is some permeability to the type of sales we will introduce.

> *"Sings a different [song] every year. It's got to be a pretty boring life, hasn't it, being a hat? I suppose it spends all year making up the next one."*
> — *Ron Weasley's*

We can name three main categories of go-to-market strategy: product-led growth (value is shown), and sales led growth (value is co-developed with the prospect). The sales led growth is further divided into transactional sales, and complex/value/enterprise sales. In addition, some companies decide to launch complex/enterprise sales with the support of a product-led growth acquisition.

'I've sorted high, I've sorted low,
I've done the job through thick and thin
So put me on and you will know
Which house you should be in...'
— The Sorting Hat

Some entrepreneurs (SaaS) are nervous at the idea of complex selling, they may think it takes too long, and they do not have the patience for it. But is it really a choice that can be made by the founders or are the features of your solution making the decision for you?

'Hmm, difficult. VERY difficult. Plenty of courage, I see.
Not a bad mind, either. There's talent, oh yes. And a
thirst to prove yourself. But where to put you?'
— The Sorting Hat

Let's look into the different types of sales:

Product-Led Growth (PLG).

There are some specific conditions to launch a successful product-led growth go-to-market strategy.

1. Your solution must be simple and easy to use. It must have a super-friendly user interface and be self-explanatory. If you believe you must create a video, or a step-by-step online tutorial, think of what you could change to avoid this requirement. Any complication can affect your conversion. Some people (many, in fact) do not have enough patience to go through a tutorial.

2. Your solution must solve a significant problem immediately. The key word is 'immediately'. Without it, the struggle of adoption begins. You must create the enthusiasm and passion your community needs from the very beginning to make your solution viral and grow. (thus avoiding heavy $ spent on ads, for example, which may not convert due to 1 &2)

3. In most cases, consider and understand that the bridge to an enterprise sale can be long and complex. (Amazon Web Services and Datadog managed it, but it took several years to build).

With the PLG strategy, you may consider a freemium/premium approach when launching a Product led Growth Strategy.

It takes a good deal of thinking ahead to launch a PLG Go to Market Strategy, the reason for which I would be putting this one in Ravenclaw, the cleverest.

Transactional selling:

This type of Go To Market Strategy is reflective of a solution that is self-explanatory, though not enough to belong to the PLG category. You need an intermediary, and a good salesperson to talk to. However, your solution does not involve any service requirements to implement. The value is perceived by the prospect within a few minutes. Typically, a sales representative will conclude 10-15 transactions within this strategy, and the sales cycle is no longer than 2 months. There is an intense rhythm associated with transactional selling.

You need a well-honed inbound and outbound lead machine to feed the volume needs. The average size deal in ARR (annual recurring revenue) is usually 5-15k with a mid-market focus.

For it is a restless job to swing so many deals a month, the sales in transactional selling below to Hufflepuff, where hard workers are most worthy of admission.

Last but not least, let's look into the one many people dread and fear the infamous complex/enterprise selling.

Are you afraid of what you'll hear?
Afraid I'll speak the name you fear?
Not Slytherin! Not Gryffindor!
Not Hufflepuff! Not Ravenclaw!
Don't worry, child, I know my job,
You'll learn to laugh, if first, you sob.
— The Sorting Hat

Complex/enterprise selling:

This is the typical route when the solution's value (product/tool) is not obvious to your prospects, it takes time to educate, and it takes time for them to understand where you will change their game. In addition, implementing your solution can take several weeks, which can include the necessity to understand the issues, the ecosystem, the scoping, and the definition of use cases.

In complex selling, you cannot manage your P&L right if you do not sell high, simply because your sales cycle is long (minimum 4-6 months). This is why it is imperative to understand the customer's problems, have them verbalized, and see whether or not you can solve them better than anyone else and how. It requires finesse, strategy, and networking. Since the sales cycle is longer, the size of the deals must be larger, and if it's done well, much more significant, even seven figures even for startups. The recommended minimum Annual recurring revenue should be $100-150k in ARR for mid-market and/or large accounts.

Complex does not mean 'difficult' but knowing how to play with several elements: initiating the interest by leveraging expert conversation around shared issues within the industry, navigating the politics in a medium or large account, and penetrating the account through multiple departments and champions...You will rely upon advanced qualification methodologies (Spin, Sandler, Challenger sales) and a high Emotional Quotient!

If I were to put complex selling into a Harry Potter House, I would say that you require chivalry, bravery, and courage in facing adversity, so Gryffindor it would be!

There are a few essential elements you must master when moving forward with complex/enterprise selling, namely: Unique Selling Points (USPs) and Ideal Customer Profile (ICP).

Why are USPs essential? Why work them?

I never put my head into the technical features of the solutions I was able to sell, whether I was selling in the IT field, the Martech field, or in the cloud. And I've always done it consciously. Why?

The more I speak technically, the more my client will speak to me technically, the less I know about my product, the more I am interested in my prospect, the more I listen to his objections, the more I try to understand where they come from and his emotions.

I don't even know how you can navigate any strategy without USPs. Let's back up for a second. How can you conduct a powerful discovery meeting[6] if you do not know where and how you can win? Knowing your differentiators, the ones where you genuinely make a difference against the competition enables you to make a better and stronger discovery. You focus only on the issues you can solve. You save yourself and your

---

[6] From my point of view, the discovery never ends. There is however a common knowledge that your deal is not strong enough until you've reach the end of the first round and initial phase of discover. Refer to Popcorn for the new CEO, forecast accuracy to review sales processes and phases.

prospect time, and you are efficient. You do not need to find a list of problems. You just need a couple that is meaningful to your prospect organization that matches your USPs.

Bonus point, documenting these elements in a concise, efficient, digestible, and accessible manner will enable your revenue team to be confident on the field much faster.

Now, since you own the strategy to influence how to win, you can address who you can win with. This is what the Ideal Customer Profile (ICP) is there for. The first pillar of a solid prospecting strategy is to know which prospects are most aligned with your current situation, considering your current resources, your product maturity, and your market maturity. You want to target the companies that will be now, not the ones you want to win when your solution is more developed and when you have more supporting resources. Your search for the ideal alignment at a specific moment. It means that you will need to review your ICP every quarter as the market is changing based on economic and political factors. An industry that was not mature for your solution may suddenly become a perfect match and vice versa.

To achieve a relevant ICP it is recommended to select 5 to 8 simple criteria. The first criteria to consider are often: Size, Income, Industry/Sector, Maturity on the subject, Geography, etc.

Each of its criteria must be able to receive a score from 0 to 2.

0 = not applicable

1 = a gray area

2 = perfect match.

The exercise will be done on all the criteria followed by an 'average' column. This column will then make it possible to select the Top 10, 20, 30, and even 50, to distribute these accounts fairly.

By targeting a limited number of prospect accounts, you can focus on the quality of your approach, address more relevant interlocutors, and, thus, maximize your chances of converting high. It is the key to complex selling, not many, but high.

The most important lesson to remember is that neither your USPs nor your ICPs will ever be perfect, not the first time, not the tenth time, but it will enhance with practice and continuous improvement. The most important is to start.

"Every great wizard in history has started out as nothing more than what we are now, students. If they can do it, why not us?" - Harry Potter.

Finally, as I mentioned, some companies may have the incredible ambition to launch both a PLG and complex selling simultaneously. For that, it requires great planning and purpose, only a Slytherin heart would dare to do so.

<u>Plot summary</u>

- ❖ We can draw three Go To Market strategies: Product leg growth, transactional, complex/value selling.
- ❖ Product Led Growth requires a strong community and a viral solution that fix a problem immediately
- ❖ Transactional selling requires volumes and inbounds
- ❖ Complex selling needs a good understanding of Unique Selling Points, Problems you address better than anyone else and a study of your Ideal Customer Profile

Ready, set, action!

❖ Where do you stand? Are you giving all the efforts to your current go to market strategy? Did you think you could work on transactional but have a long sales cycle to educate your market? Do you need to reposition yourself?

❖ Do you wish to evolve from a successful Product Led Growth strategy to targeting big enterprise accounts? Start your analysis.

REVENUE ARCHITECTURE

The A Team[7]

In recent years, many companies have hired a Chief Revenue Officer (CRO). But, for most startups and scale-ups, the notion of revenue is still all about having a

---

[7] Photo by Terence Burke on Unsplash

well-oiled sales machine. In this chapter, I have revived Hannibal Smith (aka our dear CRO) and his A-team as the customer-facing departments. If you have a problem that no one else can solve - maybe you can hire the A Team. Hannibal, who loves it when a plan comes together, leads a close-knit team of elite operatives and, when he isn't going rogue to clear his team's name, things usually run pretty smoothly.

When the CRO is responsible for the leadership of the entire customer-facing team, they can define how all departments should be working towards the common goal of increasing revenue.

This includes the following non exhaustive list: enabling collaboration, strategies, and initiatives to attract prospects; converting them into customers; educating them towards a maturity matrix; upselling, cross-selling, and retaining them as long-term clients.

The representation of a well-planned job and perfectly executed mission.

In the SaaS world, closing deals is no longer enough, the notion of recurring revenue represents the survival of the company in the long run. The revenue should therefore considered from a broader perspective than 'just' closing deals:

- Repeatability - avoid the churn
- Capacity to grow and scalability: customer satisfaction at scale,
- and vision: expand the Total Addressable Market.

This path requires time to plan the strategy and execute the processes. Two things startups and scale-ups tend to overlook. Because they are too early in the process, they believe other priorities are more important, even when, all of a sudden, scaling has created a giant mess of diverging goals and conflicting KPIs. Time is always the excuse, and urgency almost always prevails over essential matters in a fast-paced environment[8].

Col. John 'Hannibal' Smith: 'Give me a minute, I'm good. Give me an hour, I'm great. Give me six months, I'm unbeatable.'

---

[8] See Chapter: Eisenhower Matrix

In the grand scheme of things, the revenue architecture is a myth. Even though I have purposefully brought to light the traits of the following stereotypes, I'd be surprised if they did not seem familiar to many.

Capt. 'Howling Mad' Murdock: [Flying the C-130] Ladies and gentlemen we are expecting some slight turbulence so please remain in your seats until the captain has turned off the fasten seatbelts sign. Don't worry boys, turbulence has never brought down a plane!'

Sales Development Representatives (SDRs/BDRs) recruits are often young, junior, and tasked with cold-calling at high volumes, must send emails with a low opening rates, and should attempt to schedule meetings. Occasionally they are tasked with account research. Rarely are they coached or routinely developed to elevate their tactics. Much like marketing, they are expected to be lead generators, and judged by volume. The top performers are often a natural combination of art and determination and tend to leave quickly to join another company that will offer them the chance to develop into an account executive role.

Sales representatives generally fall into two categories: Account Executives (AEs) and Account Managers (AMs). Account Executives look for new prospects and Account Managers inherit open and existing accounts. This way, AEs have the responsibility to chase new logos. They are under pressure to build pipeline and close deals. For the sake of time, their account knowledge is minimal at best. When a salesperson is given a territory a prioritization of the accounts is immediately expected. However, this task is too often completed with lack of information/data and complete gut feel. At best, the existing deals in the sales pipeline will be considered as well as previous interactions, and insights from the managers. When this data is unavailable, then it is primarily gut feeling.

Col. John 'Hannibal' Smith: 'Overkill is underrated.'

AMs are under pressure to renew and scale their accounts. For them, account plans are mandatory, which are often cumbersome, I have seen powerpoint presentation over fifty slides which is a waste of time building them and lack of efficiency to use them. Rare are the ones who look into previous contracts to understand how they can align with their customer business strategies and plan expansion with their customer success. Most Customer Success Managers are scared of sales messing up their customer satisfaction.

Capt. 'Howling Mad' Murdock: [after setting Face's arm on fire] 'You're dangerous, I like you!

Pre-sales/ Sales consultants/Solution Consultants (SCs)/**Sales engineers** (SE) are the bait. SDRs, AEs and AMs will offer the prospect the possibility of a demo of their *tool*[9] for lack of better ideas of a next step. The SCs find themselves in the uncomfortable position of showing a *tool* with a standard demo (that could honestly be pre recorded). Thus, creating absolutely no added value for the prospect since there is no attachment to the solution for their technical issues.

SCs also suffer from last-minute Request For Proposal (RFP) responses they know nothing about and deliver Proof Of Concepts (POC) for which the client executive team is unaware.

---

[9] The word Tool is purposefully used here as a caricature of what should be avoided at all cost when selling software in a complex/value selling environment. You are a solution to a problem, not a hammer.

Most companies do not leverage their SC's incredible skills. The SC's job should not stop at the demo, in fact their job should not start at the demo.

As I have mentioned many times before: no pain no gain. No problem, no urgency to solve it. However, getting access to the problem for an Account Executive (AE) might be more difficult than it seems. A sales engineer brings more knowledge of operational issues, more stories, and more operational champions to break the ice and assist the AE in building a solid suitcase of problems. The SCs can, and should, be a true partner in the discovery process.

Furthermore, if the SCs is implicated in the discovery, they will be empowered to build custom demos that will resonate with the prospect. They will be telling them how they can solve their problems better than anyone else.

My recommendation to your organization is to favor a strong collaboration between AEs/AMs and SCs. They are the key essence to your success.

SCs should be curious, and avoid blaming a poor discovery. They should support, enable and empower the sales team to do better when it is not enough.

This, however, can only work when executives and leadership do not push for demos too quickly (in B2B complex sales). You should make sure the team has the time to build value. If you do this, your sales cycle will accelerate.

Sgt. Bosco 'B.A.' Baracus: 'The only reason I don't kick y'all asses is 'cause y'all outrank me.'

Customer success often inherits the garbage of poorly qualified deals with no executive commitment. Although this may sound like a stereotype, years of bad behaviors in sales have led to poor reputation. I have witnessed many customer success team dispising the sales team. Measured on renewals, churn rate[10], and NPS score, they must create intimacy with the customers by being at their beck and call after-hours, fixing issues and resolving disappointments that they did not create. Consequently, it is natural that when an

---

[10] 'Avoid the Churn' Popcorn for the New CEO

account manager asks for an introduction to the customer, they perceive it as a red alert.

"Howling Mad" Murdock: *'You guys should see these bullets in 3D! It's like we're actually being shot at!'*
B.A. Baracus: *'We are getting shot at you crazy ass fool!'*

Last but not least: a CRO without an Operations officer and partner will struggle in maintaining an operating rhythm. They will also struggle to manage their progress through data, make informed decisions and implement them back into their processes.

Lt. Templeton 'Faceman' Peck: *'Lynch is a paradox. He's a guy who needs animosity, but he loves theatricality. He's an administrator, he's not an operator. So he stays as far away from the point of impact as possible, and never gets his hands dirty if he can help it. But we're gonna change all that.'*

What is the ideal revenue architecture then?

Complete understanding of each role and alignment of their objectives and KPIs.

- AEs understand the typical pains their company can fix and align their prospecting efforts on look-alike prospects of their existing top spenders to serve them in the best way possible.

- AMs start by reviewing existing contracts and conditions, understanding them, seeking explanations, researching the current business strategies, meeting with all the tech and service partners of their accounts before meeting the customer.

- AEs & AMs consistently transfer this knowledge to the SDRs to help them understand the prospecting strategy: **who** do we target, **why**, and coach them **how**. After all, aren't sales supposed to do some active prospecting as well?

- SDRs feel entirely aligned with their AE/AM counterpart in penetrating accounts, winning customers, learning from their seniority, and gaining confidence.

- Pre Sales/ Sales Consultants are actively participating in the discovery process, deepening their understanding of the prospect's issues and crafting the technical requirements to fix them.

- Customer success receives a comprehensive and detailed briefing on **why** the customer has bought the company solution. The storytelling allows the customer to strongly onboard the new customer and craft a success plan in alignment.

And more: the marketing department supports sales with their prospecting strategies by focusing on the top spenders pains while the product team consistently work on crafting new unique differentiators to support a growing vision (and upsell/cross sell opportunities) while maintaining a strong foundation of the core business (fixing bugs).

Lt. Templeton "Faceman" Peck: Sorry to steal your line, sir. But I love it when a plan comes together.

Plot summary

- ❖ The SDR is not there to make appointments, they are the talent that we develop to find the pipeline and opportunities.

- ❖ Marketing is the right arm of sales, but without strategy we get variable execution.

- ❖ Customer success is not trash picking! Badly sold, difficult to transform a pumpkin into a golden carriage even for the most resourceful and smart of CSM

- ❖ The CPO is the conductor, and unfortunately, cannot always announce the good news (visionary roadmap).

- ❖ If there is technical debt, it impacts the whole chain, support and sales, such as the definition of ICPs.

<u>Ready, set, action!</u>

❖ If you lack pipeline (solid leads/opportunities), if you have a lot of churn (low renewal rate), if you have trouble forecasting correctly (when? how much?), ask yourself the question: Does my revenue chain work together?

BUSINESS PLAN & FORECAST

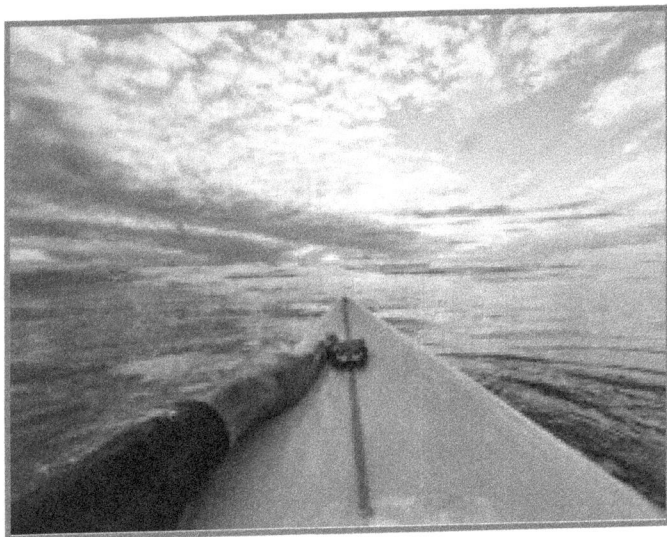

Soul Surfer

When it comes to building a business plan or facing the forecast, many entrepreneurs and Chief Revenue Officers can feel like they are in the midst of a tragedy. To bring hope, perseverance, and motivation to this particular topic, I have chosen to illustrate it with the fabulous Bethany Hamilton, a professional surfer who lost an arm to a shark attack. But returning to competition was never a question to her. The only doubt she may have faced was 'how'.

*'From the moment I caught my first wave, I knew I
wanted to be a Pro Surfer. Nothing else seemed to matter.
Surfing is my passion, my way of life. The stoke I get from
riding a perfect wave is pure joy. But like my dad always
says, life is an adventure. And sometimes you wipe out
and end up in the impact zone.'*
—— *Bethany Hamilton*

A business plan describes what you want to achieve
and how you will achieve it. It is expected to be
ambitious but nevertheless achievable: you have to give
yourself the means to achieve your ambitions: pipeline,
resources, partners, quirky and creative ideas, and
ultra-targeted focus, etc..

Pipeline assessment and setting objectives

In order to set objectives, you need to know what is
doable. Ambitious, but doable.

You must get into the CRM and start a deep analysis of
your existing pipeline. Do a proper valuation and clean
out by using qualification methodologies (Spin,
Sandler, MEDDIC, customer centric selling...). Once
you have a good idea of what your pipeline looks like

you can calculate what the gap is and figure out if your plan is achievable.

"I've learned life is a lot like surfing. When you get caught in the impact zone, you need to get right back up because you never know what's over the next wave......and if you have faith, anything is possible, anything at all."
—— *Bethany Hamilton*

Here is the guidance to your gap calculation:

STEP 1

Set your ideal objective for the year (also works at AE level by using your own quota).

Subtract anything that is 'closed won' between the beginning of the year and the overall annual objective, here I suggest 'won deals' as well as any deals in commit.

Objective (or Quota) - (closed won + commit) = Result A

The result A is the minimum amount required to **close won** to meet your annual objective.

STEP 2

Multiply Result A by your typical conversion rate (by default the complex selling industry is 3x)

Result A x Pipeline Conversion rate (default x3) =
Result B

The result B is the minimum amount of **required pipeline** to develop to have a chance of meeting your annual objective.

STEP 3

Your annual gap is, Result B minus all you already have in Upside (typically here 40%[11] and more to close). You can also subtract the existing *pipeline* here only if you have the utmost confidence in the excellence of the qualification.

Result B - (upside + qualified pipeline) = Annual gap

---

[11] Refer to Popcorn for the new CEO 1, Sales forecast accuracy

STEP 4

Knowing that from October all the pipeline created will be at risk of closing the following year, knowing that during the summer we remove 4 weeks of active prospecting, you must adjust the GAP with the seasonality:

52 weeks (if you do this the first week of the fiscal year, adjust the number based on where you are in the year) - 4 weeks of inactive prospecting over the summer - 12 weeks of last trimester going to waste = 36 weeks

STEP 5

Understand what it means weekly.

Weekly pipeline generation required = Annual
GAP/36

The number 36 will go down here as you progress through the year.

Now, look at the number based on your history of sales. Is that number doable? Is your objective too low? Too high? Achievable? And how are you going to achieve your pipeline reconciliation plan?

> *"I don't need easy, I just need possible."*
> —— *Bethany Hamilton*

Here is a quick demonstration of the calculation:

Annual Quota = $1,000,000.00
Current close won = $200,000.00
Current commit = $100,000.00
Current upside + pipeline = $400,000.00

RESULT A: Minimum required to close won

$1,000,000.00 - ($200,000.00 + $100,000.00)

=**$700,000.00**

RESULT A x (conversion rate by default x3)=
RESULT B Minimum required pipeline

$700,000.00 x 3 = **$2,100,000.00**

Result B - (upside + qualified pipeline) =
Annual GAP

$2,100,000.00 - $400,000.00 = **$1,700,000.00**

$$\textbf{Weekly} \text{ pipeline generation required} = \text{Annual}$$
$$\text{GAP}/36^{12}$$
$$\$1,700,000.00 / 36 = \$47,222.22$$

Go to Plan

You want to use the past data to understand where you can increase your average size deal while maintaining or reducing the length of your sales cycle.

You also want to draw conclusions on your ideal customer profile based on your top spenders and possible re assess with external economical and political conditions.

- Plan your outbound strategy
- Reinforce your inbound strategy and rooting of leads based on priority, ICP
- Use partners for indirect sales and boost up partnership with technological and commercial partners.

---

[12] Remember to change the week number based on where you stand in your fiscal year, 36 is an example if you were to start on week 1, as you progress, the number of weeks go down.

- Shock and awe. Don't do marketing the way you have always done it. It is time to shake up the department with creative ideas.

I was born to surf. This is why I wake up at the crack of dawn everyday. This is why I endure belly rashes, reef cuts and muscles so tired they feel like needles.
—— *Bethany Hamilton*

Adaptability

Your Business Plan is not perfect. You will have to work hand in hand with operations to measure the results (build a list of KPIs) regularly (weekly and monthly). Churn rate, creation of pipeline/rep/region, average size deal, closing time, number of up-sells, number of cross-sells, number of new logos, number of new meetings, number of partner meetings, number of sells-through, etc. Monitor the success of the plan, adjust as needed, adapt and communicate on the progress made.

Cheri Hamilton: You can't just fix everything just by sheer will.

Tom Hamilton: If she gives up, she will never get back into the water and she will never be the same.

Last but not least, **the forecast** will impact your business plan and your Profit & Loss Statement. The forecast is the pondered collection of your qualified pipeline, upside, commits and renewals. It is your revenue prediction. A continuous analysis of the revenue risks (new + renewal) allows the capacity to forecast with accuracy. Typically, in complex selling, we call forecast accuracy a revenue generated at the end of the quarter that is no more than +/- 5%, of the forecasted number at the beginning of the quarter.

Depending on the forecast, the CFO can make various decisions that will impact the Profit & Loss Statement such as recruiting, making an acquisition, investing in new locations when the forecasted revenue shows growth and positivity. Yet if you come short of what has been predicted, the impact to the company can be disastrous, you might need to lay off employees, relocate, close offices and more.

Alternatively, the CFO could decide to avoid expenses due to a short forecast. You could then miss out on a great acquisition opportunity, he could also decide on a hiring freeze and miss out on talent. But what happens if the revenue comes way above the forecast? These opportunities to spend the money are gone.

Forecast accuracy goes both ways, too low and you miss out, too high and you are at risk.

The danger of the forecast therefore lies in its lack of precision and risk management!

Plot summary

- ❖ Business Plan is the objective you set yourself to achieve and how.
- ❖ Forecast requires accuracy, what you say you are going to bring in should be within the 95%-105% range.
- ❖ A Business Plan cannot be successful without a close monitoring of the current Pipeline and the weekly/annual GAP.

Ready, set, action!

- ❖ How did you set your objective for the year? Is it realistic? Have you shared it with all departments? Are you working on a plan to achieve it together?
- ❖ What is your forecast accuracy? How often do you monitor it?
- ❖ What is your Pipeline GAP? What is your plan to overcome it? How will you support the sales team to achieve it?

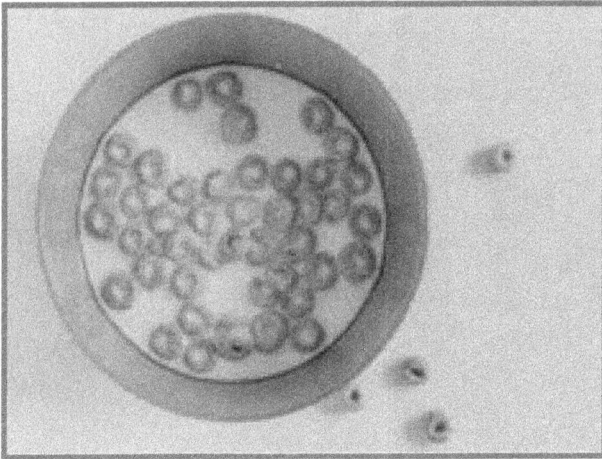

Honey I shrunk the kids[13]

This chapter was co written with the incredible Jenny Herald, VP of Product Evangelism at Quantive. I am incredibly thankful to how she has embedded her expertise and skills in this chapter.

OKRs, 'Objective key results,' most famously adopted by Google, have a long history, harking Intel back in 1968. Nowadays, the startup world is divided. Should you, or should you not, implement them?

---

[13] Photo by freestocks on Unsplash

Initially, the main objectives behind implementing OKRs within a company were:

1. Achieving strategic alignment
2. Focusing on execution
3. Engaging employees
4. Setting an operating rhythm for execution

Yet, somehow, whether by lack of expertise or lack of experience, their implementation tends to be somewhat chaotic, often confusing, and as companies scale, divisive. A relatively similar feeling to what Szalinski's kids may have experienced as their dad's innovation shrunk them to the size of a cheerio cereal.

Amy Szalinski: 'If you were my brother, I'd put myself up for adoption.'

The first mistake young companies make when setting OKRs is to disregard their ultimate corporate objective. What do they want to achieve? And by when? Setting quarterly OKRs necessitates the inclusion of a long-term vision. You need to provide your employees with time and perspective to engage in strategic execution and make a meaningful business impact.

Russell 'Russ' Thompson, Sr.: 'Hey, Szalinski, your lawn's beginning to look like the Amazon.'

Wayne Szalinski: 'Yeah, producing oxygen, Russ. We all have to do our part. You know how all the jungles are receding everywhere.'

Lack of structure around what they do and what they mean is why OKRs are adored by some and loathed by others; why they work exceptionally well for some companies – but can be a complete failure for others.

Amy Szalinski: 'Mud is still mud, no matter how small you are.'

Even if you do not choose to implement OKRs, you still need your business strategies to be coherent and in complete alignment with execution. What should you do then? How can you ensure their successful deployment?

First, make sure to align everyone on your company's corporate objective; this is the call to which all employees, no matter their department or title, must respond. Setting this true north is critical whether you decide to deploy OKRs or not.

Most startups and scale-ups corporate objectives in their early stages point towards increasing revenue. However, you may also have a long-term vision – such as being the leader of your field or being the most complete platform out there.

Communicating this clearly and repeatedly is essential, especially as you scale. You may think your employees know – but don't assume. Not all that happens in board meetings should be disclosed – but to ensure the smooth execution of your business plan, a minimum should be so your employees understand pivots when they happen.

Amy Szalinski: 'I don't think we're in Kansas anymore, Toto.'
Nick Szalinski: 'I don't think we're in the food chain anymore, Dorothy.'

Second, once your corporate objective is clear and transparent to all, align your executives on the key business strategies your company should implement to support it.

Each department will then define its own supporting initiatives. Such initiatives will require resources; before moving forward with defining and putting in place quarterly OKRs, ensure that budget allocation, constraints, P&L management, and hiring requirements are transparent, understood, and ready to be deployed. Do this, no matter your company's size or stage – whether you are 5 people starting out, 50 and growing, or 500 and scaling, the process remains the same.

Professor Frederickson: 'Mr Szalinski, are you trying to tell me that suddenly size is no longer relative?'

The purpose of implementing OKRs within an organisation is to enable collaborators to shift their mindset from activity/output thinking to outcome/impact thinking. Teams can get so caught up in delivery, they build features that create no value. Orienting around OKRs eliminates needless work. It puts the customer in the center of everything you do.

Now, the notion of KPIs vs OKRs is often discussed. People ask how they're different. KPIs can exist without OKRs, but generally OKRs cannot exist without KPIs.

KPIs are 'health' metrics that help you understand how your organization is performing. They are monitored regularly to ensure that your business performance targets are achieved and maintained. OKRs help you set, track, and update ambitious, measurable, and time-bound goals. The truth is, they are complementary.

It's highly likely your KPIs will be the same quarter after quarter, possibly year after year. OKRs, on the other hand, will adapt and change as your priorities change. Let's say you monitor website traffic as one of your KPIs. You see that traffic on your website is going well. You know a lot of your sales come through your website. Therefore, driving quality traffic to your website is crucial. You might set an OKR like this:

Objective: Drive quality traffic to our website

Key Result 1: Increase website visitors from X to Y

Key Result 2: Keep bounce rate below Z

Key Result 3: Ensure average session duration is above A

Russel, Russ Thompson Jr. 'Hey, if we had some rope, we could make a log bridge! If we... If we had some logs.'

When it comes to sales, targets tend to relate exclusively around the compensation plan – e.g., the number of new logos, number of deals signed above-average ARR, and so on. When it comes to marketing, we measure leads or 'marketing qualified' leads, but how are these metrics really connected? How do they synchronize your departments rather than divide them?

So, what should you put in place? Shared OKRs. Shared OKRs are an effective tool to create alignment between different teams or functions. They exist to solve dependencies. With shared OKRs, everyone is committed to achieving a goal in the same period of time. Teams are pushed to aspire, stretch, and not fear failure. It is important to make clear that OKRs will not be directly tied to compensation. OKR achievement might be an input into employee performance evaluations, but isn't everything. You want to create an environment where employees work hard for intrinsic reasons such as fulfilling the mission.

Determine metrics that are achievable for your departments when they're working together. Often I see OKRs chosen independently, which end up having the opposite results to those intended. Departments shouldn't end up working against one another!

Ron Thompson:'It's just that my dad doesn't understand your dad.'
Amy Szalinski: 'Your dad doesn't understand anything.

Plot summary
- ❖ OKRs are a means to an end, they help put things in motion, execute on your corporate objective, business strategies and initiatives
- ❖ OKRs should not create confusion. Be transparent with your goal and strategies, create alignment between departments and functions through shared goals
- ❖ Align remuneration and KPIs accordingly, provide time for your teams and employees to be successful in delivering on the initiatives.

<u>Ready, set, action!</u>

❖ Why do you want to put OKRs in place? What do you intend to achieve?

❖ How engaged are your employees to the success of your company?

❖ How confident are you that all your departments are in sync to deliver on your business objective?

❖ How transparent is your internal communication?

EISENHOWER MATRIX

The devil wears Prada

As a company scales, a complex organization settles in—one with too many meetings, where everything seems to be both urgent and important. Many people will tell you that joining a startup is like taking a bullet train.

Miranda Priestly: 'Truth is, there is no one who can do what I do'

Andrea Sachs must have felt a similar feeling when joining Miranda Priestly, editor-in-chief of *Runway* magazine, as her junior personal assistant in 'The Devil Wears Prada'. But, as much as you may be able to run fast - in trainers or Chanel boots - working for a startup is not a sprint. It is a marathon.

Miranda: 'By all means, move at a glacial pace. You know how that thrills me.'

The rise of social media and instant messaging has increased this perception. Digital technology makes it seem like all requests have become equally urgent and important. The acceleration of remote work and video conferences, and the subsequent lack of breaks and fresh air, have increased our actual productivity.

We are 'always on.'

Nigel: 'Come on. Miranda's pushed the run through up a half hour. And she's always 15 minutes early.'
Andy: 'Which means?'
Nigel: 'You're already late.'

However you think you prioritize- take a second, pause, and ask yourself: are you really getting things done the way they should be?
Countless times in the last few years have I discussed the necessity to review a company's perception of time

management and the consequences to their departments and employees.

Why is it that many tasks and requests end up being both urgent and important even for the most mature executives?

Getting everything done at once, right away - and done well - is not impossible. It is merely ridiculously inefficient. Forgetting that prioritization is essential may kill your company's productivity and effectiveness in the long run.

Emily: 'You know, I rarely say this to people who... aren't me, but you have got to calm down! Bloody hell...'

Even Dwight David Eisenhower, a five-star general in the United States Army who served as Supreme Commander and was responsible for preparing the Allied invasion of Europe strategy, required prioritization management. That's why he invented the matrix named after his own name - the Eisenhower matrix.

Nevertheless, knowing about such a matrix does not mean you master it. How confident are you that you are practicing it right in your daily startup life?

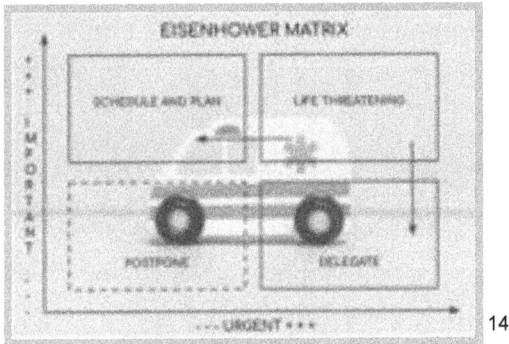

14

Let's go back to the basics – the ones that you, deep-down, know very well, but you have to read again to act upon. It's time to realize how much impact this five-minute daily exercise could have on you and your team.

Urgent: means that it requires your immediate attention. I often tell the people I work with that no position in the B2B tech startup world compares to being a heart surgeon. What does this mean? You have at least a few seconds, if not a few minutes, to decide

---

14 Photo by JOSHUA COLEMAN on Unsplash

whether a task is urgent, if you should delegate it (not important), to whom, or even to postpone it (not that urgent after all), and how.

Nigel: 'And that's my problem because... Oh, wait. No, it's not my problem.'

Important: means that the task is meaningful. Whatever it is, it will have an impact on your company's long-term vision, value, and objectives. Because of its long-term perspective, an important task requires more than one person organization, strategic thinking, and reiteration. It is therefore uncommon that such a mission be both important and urgent. Any assignment or meeting scheduled to fulfill a critical mission should always come first. It should not be postponed under any circumstances. Avoiding delegation of other lesser important tasks shows that your prioritization is wrong. Without understanding this, you'll just go through the unhelpful urgent/ important spiral again.

Emily Charlton: 'I don't care if she was going to fire you or beat you with a red hot poker. You should have said no!'

Now that we have established what is what, here is a simple plan of action:

- Not important/ not urgent: let them be, these issues usually solve themselves in time.

- Important but not urgent: long-term planning with an established rhythm. You must schedule and list all actions in your calendar with an operating rhythm.

- Not important but urgent: delegate; find someone who has the skills to focus on your own tasks.

You don't need to step in every time you are asked to do something – such as, for example, joining a last-minute meeting to save the day – yet, you do do it... Admit it.

Andy: 'That's not what I... no, that was different. I didn't have a choice.'
Miranda: 'No, no, you chose. (...) You want this life. Those choices are necessary.'

Why do you?

Because of a thing we commonly refer to as ego: a dangerous combination with this new always on, always connecting space-time continuum we live in.

News flash: having a busy schedule does not mean you are essential. Having ten meetings per day does not mean you are efficient nor productive. Make the choices that matter to make a difference; make yourself impactful.

How do you avoid getting in that crazy spiral then?

- Color-code your calendar and fill it with blockers for fundamentals. Know and own your non-negotiable tasks: the ones you must accomplish to be productive and efficient. Schedule them weekly and never ever deviate from them.

- Reduce interactions to the actual time : do you need an hour for this meeting? Or would 45 minutes be enough? Do the same with frequency: do you need to meet every week, or would bi-weekly be enough?

- Identify requests that flatter your ego versus those that bring added value to your company goals. Will you make a difference in this last-minute meeting that is entirely unprepared, or will you lose time? Should you fix this line of code or recruit to avoid being understaffed?

Miranda: 'Find me that piece of paper I had in my hand yesterday morning.'

If this seems straightforward and easy enough for you, you may want to check your whole team and apply these 'simple' principles. You may be surprised by what is going on within your company, department or team.

Nigel: 'Excuse me, can we adjust the attitude? Don't make me feed you to one of the models.'

Plot summary

- ❖ Urgent is rarely important.
- ❖ Important cannot be delegated.
- ❖ Failure to see the difference puts you and your company at risk of executing your mid term and long term strategy properly.
- ❖ Whatever you think you are doing right, stop, pause and reflect, you can improve your operating rhythm.

Ready, set, action!

- ❖ How often do you do the exercise of the matrix, put your actions into the Eisenhower matrix templates?
- ❖ What actions could you have delegated last week?
- ❖ What important projects must you accomplish? What is your operating rhythm to make it happen? Do you ever deviate from it?

TECHNICAL DEBT MANAGEMENT

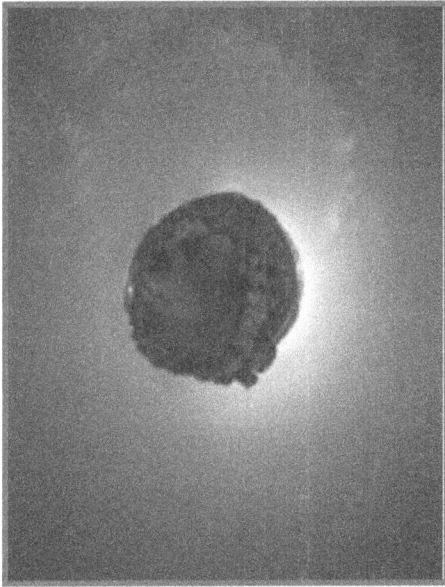

Don't look up[15]

'Don't look up' is a movie produced and distributed by Netflix that portrays our capacity to be indifferent to what matters and, in this case, an allegory to climate change. Because the entire movie is a satire of our society and pushes us to open our eyes, this chapter's objective is to show you how ignoring your technical debt might just cost you your company.

---

[15] Photo by Bryan Goff on unsplash

Or, as Randall Mindy would say: 'This will affect the entire planet.'

No matter how hard you try, it is very likely that your company will face a technical debt at some point.

Its origins can vary:
- a competitive landscape,
- difficulties in hiring developers,
- sudden change in leadership,
- high spender customers requiring specific features,
- a bug tsunami without ever finding the origin of it all,
- a constant roadmap deviation to please new customers.

At this stage, it could very well be a mix of it all, and finding the right person or department to blame is useless.

It would be too simplistic to say that technical debt is owned by the technical team, much like it is too simplistic to say that revenue is simply owned by the sales team.

A sales team that has an average product cannot be successful.

A technical team that constantly deviates from its plan to satisfy ad hoc requests from the sales team and customer success team cannot be successful either.

Symptoms of the technical debt are as follows:

- The roadmap is not delivering any new features and is not planning on doing so in the next 12 months.
- The roadmap is catching up with essential features to keep up with the market.
- The product roadmap is no longer visionary nor inspiring (no differentiators)
- Churn is increasing due to low customer satisfaction (too many tickets linked to software issues unresolved)
- The sales pipeline is slowing down.
- Deals are won on false promises.
- Historical partners find new software vendors in your competitive landscape to partner with?

And more.

These symptoms, individually taken, are not necessarily a representation of the technical debt but they sure are a strong diagnosis of it when combined.

Kate Dibiasky: 'I have news for you. It's already a complete disaster.'

Unfortunately, by the time symptoms have occurred, the sales, marketing, and customer success department have already been launching missiles at an overloaded, overworked, and exhausted technical team.

The sales department complains that the solution is not unique enough and that their customers' requests are not considered. The sales will wrongly assume that this is why they cannot sign new clients.

The customer success latches out, exhausted from facing unsatisfied customers who cannot get an answer on how and when their issue in the software/platform/solution will be fixed.

The marketing department can no longer take the pressure of generating new leads with three years old messaging and outdated value propositions.

Randall Mindy: 'How do we even talk to each other? What've we... What've we done to ourselves? How do we fix it?'

The most important and difficult step is to admit as early as possible that the technical debt is present. Before symptoms occur, identify the warnings. Find a plan to overcome it, and communicate appropriately.

Randall Mindy: "Not everything needs to sound so clever, charming, or likable all the time. Sometimes we need just to be able to say things to one another. We need to hear things." -

Sometimes the easiest route is the one to take. In all the symptoms and frustrations, we notice that all the departments have objectives in silos. They work together within their team but not *ensemble* towards a common goal for the company.

The technical team must bring visibility and transparency to the challenges the team is facing. If the technical debt is, in fact, occurring, it is essential to explain what it means in simple terms, understandable by all. No lies, no bullshit. If the team needs eighteen months to get back on the visionary track, then this is the timeline that should be communicated. Ignoring, masking, or lying about the issue will only fester the situation even further. This will enable the customer-facing departments to devise a plan to protect the technical team by stepping up on the frontline and knowing what should be done.

Randall Mindy: 'As long as you do the right thing. We're there for you.'

Here is what each department could do:

Sales should be able to work a new ideal customer profile based on the current product maturity and push back on filling out requests for proposals that are not a match. Furthermore, prospects will always ask for a special feature that has no impact on their business, and it is important to educate the customer on how little importance this feature would have. However, remaining open to suggestions is important as some key features with maximum impact on the business could be considered in the roadmap, especially if they align with the plan to fix the technical debt or require just a few man-days.

The customer success department is on the frontline. Customers can scream for bugs that have little to no impact on the overall usage and/or the business. It is essential to take the time to talk, qualify, interrogate and challenge the customer to filter out which ones are the most impactful at scale. This will enable an arbitrage team (or product owner) to assess the situation better and faster so the development team does not get lost in a tsunami of requests.

Marketing should support the entire company by focusing on the solution strengths, the stories of clients that have confirmed their trust and engagement, and boost the messaging around problems that need solving rather than features and functions. The marketing team should also play an essential role in supporting the definition of the most accurate Ideal Customer Profile (ICP), one that belongs to the value proposition of today without overselling or overreaching.

Kate Dibiasky: 'I will be 100% behind this effort. No matter how offensive I may find you.'

In essence, you've understood it. The key is communicating openly about the issue so the entire company can work *ensemble* towards a common global objective. The company can therefore maintain and grow the revenue while giving time and space to the technical team to deliver on the debt and work on a new visionary roadmap.

Randall Mindy: "Everything is theoretically impossible until it is done"

<u>Plot summary</u>

- ❖ Acknowledge a potential technical debt before symptoms occur.

- ❖ Typical symptoms: lack of vision in the roadmap, catching up on essential features, overworked technical team, churn and lack of sales pipeline.

- ❖ Transparency, communication and plan visibility are essential to overcome a moment that is frustrating.

- ❖ Revenue and technical debt are the responsibility of all, not just of the typical associated departments: sales for revenue, tech for technical debt.

<u>Ready, set, action!</u>

- ❖ Do you do pulse surveys with your teams? How do you get insights on frustrations before symptoms occur?
- ❖ When a CTO or CPO major change occurs, how do you manage the negative consequences of the necessary time to adapt? How transparent are you?
- ❖ How often do you measure the churn? How do you associate bugs unresolved to customer satisfaction? How do you give yourself and your customer time to fix the issues?
- ❖ How often do you give a clear, transparent visibility on the vision (roadmap are often hidden from customer facing departments for fear of false promises to the client)

BOOK II:
PEOPLE DEEP DIVE

MINDSET & VALUABLE TIME

Fight club[16]

80% of the outcome of a meeting depends on how well you prepare for it. This situation is especially true if there's an evident power dynamic between meeting attendees – for example, in the boardroom.

There are three typical outcomes: frustrated attendees, excited attendees, or, worst of all, unmoved attendees. The last thing you want is for people to leave feeling

[16] Photo by Mathew MacQuarrie on Unsplash

blank —as if nothing had happened and no valuable exchange had taken place.

To maximize your chance of creating a positive outcome from any meetings, position all the issues you face out in the open from the start. From a general perspective, by laying out the struggles you are facing from the beginning and asking them for their guidance, you put the participants at ease to bring you creative insights, solutions, and value.

No great brainstorming session ever arose from a perfect situation, so let's put up a gentle fight. To illustrate my point, I'll be enlisting the help of the famous Tyler Durden, the Fight Club's Narrator.

Tyler Durden: 'It's only after we've lost everything that we're free to do anything.'

Let's look at the common mistakes and states of mind that we can highlight during the preparation phase of an important meeting :

(Hardly) Preparing at the last minute and hoping for the best.

Confusing, urgent and important meetings lead us to believe the phase of preparation is a waste of time. This situation will often occur due to poor past experience: the previous meetings were held in a disorganized way, jumping from one subject to another, with little structure or guidance, thus providing little value and no call to actions. Without an agreement on follow-ups, there was no tracking of progress until the next meeting, which most probably repeated precisely in the same manner.

The usual downside is that encounters will become more and more scarce, using poor excuses for rescheduling, postponing, and canceling.

Narrator: 'Most people... normal people... do just about anything to avoid a fight.'

To postpone any conflicts, you put up a presentation with a few graphics, promising things that, deep down, know will happen fictitiously. Your objective is to get out of the meeting as soon as possible, head high – with a few pumped-up figures and a fluffy plan.

Tyler Durden: 'Sticking feathers up your butt does not make you a chicken.'

Preparing thoroughly with details

Some spend so much time gathering information that they get lost in details. Time is of the essence, and gathering information from different sources is critical but should not be cumbersome. You must know what to ask, how to structure it, and how to use it efficiently. Too much information can lose your audience, ruin a meeting and its positive expected outcome.

Tyler Durden: 'Man, I see in Fight Club the strongest and smartest men who've ever lived. I see all this potential, and I see it squandered.'

Iit is a double punishment: the person has put a lot of effort into the preparation but, because of a lack of focus on the essence, misses the opportunity to get valuable feedback, strategic suggestions, and actionable insights. This situation leaves a bittersweet taste in the mouths of everyone attending. Because no clear ask has been presented to the brains in the room, additional work – actions that have nothing to do with the situation – is dished out. The feeling of misunderstanding is mutual.

Chuck Palahniuk: 'If you don't know what you want,' the doorman said, 'you end up with a lot you don't.'

Assessing the issues, presenting a plan, providing clear asks.

Now, this approach seems simple enough – and is the most logical way to address a meeting. Nevertheless, it is the hardest to execute on. Many people feel a need to justify they've done enough – to prove to others and themselves they are doing their job correctly.

This meeting style requires a person who feels confident enough to be vulnerable, lay out the missing piece of the puzzle and ask others for help. They're willing to put their ego to the side and accept being challenged without feeling bruised.

Tyler Durden: 'Today is the sort of day where the sun only comes up to humiliate you.'

It takes an extraordinary amount of courage, a positive mindset, and a coachable mind to present the issues - the gap to accomplishing a plan - as a meeting agenda. Yet, this way of doing things is the most effective one to move forward and extract value from the brilliant minds surrounding you.

Since the challenges are primarily laid out, it avoids a lengthy conversation to uncover them, leaving space for the people around the table to provide additional problem-solving ideas and a clear path of actions to achieve a solution. Providing an accomplished plan to be reviewed will grant you a successful meeting and a good reputation.

Tyler Durden: 'How's that working out for you?'
Narrator: 'What?'
Tyler Durden: 'Being clever.'
Narrator: 'Great.'
Ricky: 'Keep it up then.'

Don't forget to provide attendees with a list of actions to accomplish after the meeting ends.

In a properly conducted board meeting, you might collectively decide it is time to kill a demanding product with little impact or let go of a team member or an executive that is no longer a fit for your organization.

If you don't do this – you'll find yourself alone in the decision and execution process.

Chuck Palahniuk: 'I don't want to die without any scars.'

In conclusion, when you put yourself in the defender's position as, for example, justifying your plan of action, you naturally put the other people in the attacker's place. If you want a sparring partner, don't consider your hierarchy, board, or customer as superior. You owe them respect, but this is won by bringing value, structure, and expertise to the fight.

Whether you're present to your board, your leadership, your manager, or your customer, when the notion of revenue is involved, addressing the gap with all your might is the most efficient and effective route. Those who have applied all of these principles form part of a particular club.

But shhh, we can't talk about it.

A sales organization often refers to its failures, successes, recruitment, objectives, and more in terms of elite sports. Success is not just about acquiring hard skills. It is about training the soft skills with consistency, testing your will and discipline, and learning new hard skills when you've mastered the old ones.

If you are looking to build an A team with A players, you will stumble upon questions like what skills should I be looking to create a solid foundation?

JB Bernstein: 'How fast do they pitch in cricket? I think I cracked this.'
Ash: 'They don't play baseball in India.'
JB Bernstein: 'That's right. They don't. They play cricket. But we think that we can convert a cricket bowler into a baseball pitcher.'

When it comes to assessing soft skills, few will hit the home run without the four below categories (DICE: Drive, Intelligence, Coachability, Experience):

Drive: Someone who is training for a marathon has the will to achieve an objective and the discipline to do it.

"Build a culture that rewards—not punishes—people for getting problems into the open where they can be solved."
—— *Ben Horowitz*

<u>Plot summary</u>

❖ The outcome of a meeting depends on the mindset you set for it. Your history with the interlocutors should be put aside.

❖ No preparation always leads to chaos and little follow up call to actions (or unwanted tasks)

❖ You can get lost into details, prepare but avoid over preparation.

❖ The best meetings are the one where you have previously identified the issues you are facing, you share them with your peers/or leadership and position your ask to solve the problem.

❖ A meeting must have a follow up plan/action.

<u>Ready, set, action!</u>

- ❖ Are all your meetings necessary? Can some of them be replaced by structured communication?

- ❖ Are you currently satisfied with how your meetings are held? Do you feel you have received valuable insights, feedback and energy?

SOFT SKILLS, HARD SKILLS & WILL

Million Dollar Arm

The Walt Disney motion picture *Million Dollar Arm* based on the true story of two young Indians, Rin Singh, and Dinesh Patel, who are discovered by American sports agent, J.B Bernstein.

J.B had the bold idea of exploring the possibili bringing a cricket player into Major League Baseba

Look for people who consistently push themselves out of their comfort zone, people who don't need others to set objectives for them. They are the ones who will not take a quota as a final goal but as a minimum requirement to achieve.

Intelligence: Do they have the capacity to make the best use of their time? The ability to assess urgent vs. important? Can they quickly learn about your process, your solution, the problems you solve and your use cases?

Coachability: This is the most important one, if someone has too much ego or listens but is incapable of applying your advice, you cannot help that kind of individual's personal growth.

Experience: A resume is only part of the story. Experience can be acquired outside of school and outside of typical career paths. Explore their stories, what did they learn from their mistakes, failures, what would they do differently? Someone who does not learn from experience cannot adapt.

Mastering these categories will enable your organization to recruit better, allow successful transfers from one department to another in your organization and justify promotions.

JB Bernstein: 'We go over there and find these guys; we bring them back here, we train them in LA. Get them ready in a year'

The hiring situation: Often, the recruitment process is rushed. Indeed, too many things in business are rushed, from making the decision to hire and reducing onboarding time to expecting instant performance.

For Rinku Singh and Dinesh Patel, trust was essential. Being under pressure as soon as they set foot in America was counterproductive to their performance. In sales, most salespeople have the pressure to close their first deal within 3 to 6 months, and when they don't, the pressure increases exponentially.

My advice is to take more time to make the right choices, then support, back them up and develop them so that they can be the best versions of themselves. One way of doing this is to give them existing qualified opportunities to learn on the field, close a deal and nail their first success. Feeling trusted goes a long way.

Coach House: 'Cricket and baseball are two completely different throwing motions. The biomechanics, the timing, the sequencing, it's just not the same at all.'

The transferee situation: Can a Customer Success or a Solution Consultant become an Elite Salesperson? Can someone from a completely different career as a high level consultant become an Elite salesperson? Changing roles requires adaptation. Taking the time to set up a proper transition with mentors and support is essential for a transferee to thrive.

J.B Bernstein: 'Sometimes to win, you have to change the game.'

The promoted situation: From being a Sales Development Representative to becoming an Account Executive (AE), from being an AE to stepping up in a manager role, soft skills are important, and determination is essential. Do not step into a role unprepared. You must train and seek mentoring, coaching and readings to prepare for your next job.

Prior to your promotion, acquire the hard skills before you have to do it, learn and experience, set yourself up for success by avoiding having too many skills to learn at once.

From the leadership perspective, running a skill/will assessment is essential which you can start by listing open-ended questions such as: How would you describe your strengths in your current role? How will you make a difference in your future position? What would prevent you from being successful in your role/next role? How excited are you about your day-to-day job? What is boring you in your current role? etc.

Formalizing this process in a skill/will matrix, scoring not only the eagerness for the current and next positions as well the hard skills to acquire is a good way to define a career path and development plan whether you are hiring, transferring or promoting a person. This delicate balance is often shaken up in the tech startup and scale-up world. Take the time to talk about this once a quarter, away from Quarterly Business Reviews (QBR) and standard Objectives Key Results (OKRs) settings.

Setting a clear development path with milestones, allocating people committed to the person's success, focusing on trust, and lowering the pressure to deliver in the first few months will maximize your chances of success.

Last but not least, how do you find your own Rinku Singh and Dinesh Patel? As mentioned before, setting up the right environment is key. If you want someone's personality to shine, they need to be themselves, and for that, they need to feel comfortable. Create a setup where people feel a little less under the microscope and a little more into a friendly conversation.

You are looking for the following critical elements in their personal story:

Drive: What are they passionate about? Do they have hobbies that sparkle their eyes when they talk about it? How dedicated are they?

Intelligence: Do they consistently want to learn? Are they readers? Podcast listeners? How fast can they adapt to new situations? What is their emotional intelligence? Do they have empathy?

All of these elements are only pointers. If you want to see the real personality of your candidates, you must take the time to know them, it may seem like a time investment at the moment, but it will save you from making a mistake.

Coachability: What were their biggest failures? Are they presenting them in ways it shows learning? What are their biggest successes? Are they referring to other people in their stories? Are they grateful?

Experience: What was the most challenging time in their lives, and how did they act, react and cope? Create a puzzle that needs solving, a case, and have them work it out with other candidates. Are they leveraging each other? Are they competing? What is most crucial, solving or shining?

Some culture hates this, but you can also name a speed meeting hour when your candidates meet people from all departments at 5 minutes interval. Collecting the interviewers' first impressions will provide you with additional key insights.

Plot summary

❖ There are four soft skills essential to a great salesperson: intelligence, coachability, drive and experience.

❖ A regular Soft skills assessment is critical to operate the business and ensure your people's success.

❖ Providing the means, resources and mentorship to achieve success is as important as the identification of the soft skills.

Ready, set, action!

❖ How do you recruit? What are you looking for? How do you prepare a transferee or a promotion? How smooth is the path to performance?

❖ How do you train your hiring managers and HR to assess, monitor and develop soft skills within your organization?

THE ROLE OF THE SALES LEADER

Invictus[17]

Many founders lack a background in sales. They can get past the MVP stage, winning their first customers, but when a startup scales, the art, passion, and dedication of a CEO are no longer enough to scale the revenue for profitability.

---

[17] Photo by Igor Eberling on Unsplash

Nelson Mandela: 'Times change. We need to change as well.'

When the need for scale appears, co-founders tend to hunt for exceptional talent to help everyone deliver. But, is providing deals the only thing you should expect from a sales leader? What are the top five things they should excel in?

Pipeline and growth

A sales leader will create a robust pipeline. The first mistake you want to avoid is to hire an expensive sales leader because of their network. A sales leader inspires and coaches their team in being creative and finding new ways of hunting deals; whether by leveraging their knowledge of the market, grabbing a few speakers at the end of an event, or spending time thinking about marketing – demand generation and the fundamentals of an online acquisition including the lead generation process.

While your sales leader should accompany their team in meetings, it should only be to support development, never to sell on their behalf.

François Pienaar: 'I think he wants us to win the World Cup'

Forecasting

MEDDIC[18] is not the sole methodology out there to manage a forecast. It is, however, an undeniably powerful framework when it comes to conducting a diagnostic and a list of meaningful calls-to-actions. You should expect your sales leader to forecast accurately, quarterly and to update you weekly in the last month of the quarter. They should make a call at the beginning of the quarter accurate to within 5% of the actual closing.

Too often, a deal is forecasted based on a theme to which your company can attach for example 'the prospect wishes to engage in Digital acceleration.'

Your sales leader's role will be to understand the possible impacts of not digitilizing fast enough, such as losing revenue and market share or increasing operating costs.

---

[18] Also referred to as MEDDICC, MEDDPIC, MEDDPICC.

These negative business consequences are the motivation to find a budget allocation to your solution and a date and time to buy and avoid digitilizing delays and associated impacts.

A sales leader can see through fake deals and will be able to pivot back to the discovery phase, at the very beginning of the sales process, where necessary.

Brenda Mazibuko: 'You're risking your political capital. You're risking your future as our leader.'

Nelson Mandela: 'The day I am afraid to do that is the day I am no longer fit to lead.'

Define and execute on an 'operating rhythm.'

Execution is imperative in a dynamic sales environment. To prevent double-booking and focus on delivering successful meetings, your sales leader must define an 'operating rhythm' and set expectations before every session.

Jason Tshabalala: 'Ah, that must be Jessie with the schedule. Come in, beautiful!'

A sales leader should:

Bi-weekly:
Interact and brainstorm with peers (R&D, Customer Success, Marketing, ...)

Weekly:
Conduct a one-to-one with each sales representative, reviewing meaningful metrics such as number of meetings conducted and booked, pipeline created, forecast progression and accuracy and define actions around personal development, etc.

Conduct a forecast review using a methodology of their choice and sticking to it for each opportunity.

Organize a team meeting with a predefined and shared agenda. By choosing someone in the team to share a particular successful story, your sales leader can ensure peer-to-peer learning.

Quarterly:
Organize a territory plan and a business review to hold their team accountable for the quarter number and

delivery while committing non-sales groups and resources to support the growth and closing strategy.

Ad hoc:
Participate in keynotes and Public events and transformational projects and technology implementation such as call-recording, forecasting tools, sales automation, effective content generation, management, etc.

Recruitment
Experienced sales leaders know you need a pipeline of sales candidates as much as you need a customer pipeline because:
You might promote someone.
Someone might leave.
You might need to get rid of someone performing poorly.

And if you wait for one of these to happen to start looking for the perfect candidate, you will lose six to nine months. Being on the hunt for the perfect candidate at all times makes a good sales leader. You should not delegate the search entirely to someone else; it should always be a shared strategy. Top sales reps work hand-in-hand with their SDRs, and leading sales leaders work with their recruitment agency or internal Human Resources department to identify and convert top candidates.

Personal Development

All of this will only work if your sales leader is coachable and adaptable. The world changes at an incredible pace, and this is why you must hire someone with tremendous learning and unlearning skills.

Nelson Mandela: 'If I cannot change when circumstances demand it, how can I expect others to?'

How can you tell others what to do if you are not willing to learn, not ready to dedicate time to becoming a better version of yourself?

A sales leader should take time to read up on what others are doing, attend webinars, watch videos from peers, and have mentors. No matter what your background, there is always something new to learn. This is actually something you should expect from any member of your team no matter their level of seniority.

Nelson Mandela: 'How do you inspire your team to do their best?'

François Pienaar: 'By example. I've always thought to lead by example, Sir.'

MANAGING SALES REMOTELY

Jerry Maguire [19]

Sales, a position owned for decades by people who have easy contact with people, a job that requires intense networking and face-to-face meetings, has expanded remotely in recent years (due/thanks to Covid).

---

[19] Photo by Eric Deeran on Unsplash

From leadership to managing prospects and customers, the future of work is evolving.

In an increasingly remote environment, key leaders and sales professionals have had to reinvent their ways of creating relationships and intimacy. Much like the sales department, Jerry Maguire, one of the most important representatives of Sports Management International, used to feel like the king of the world but had to reinvent himself after being fired.

B2B prospecting has never been more digital. To address the subject of physical separation and its implications, let's look into these three categories: remote management, remote prospecting, and remote relationship building.

Locker Signs: 'A positive anything is better than a negative nothing.'

As a leader, inspiring and motivating your troops through social interactions are often essential to the well-being and thriving of your team. Invite external speakers to boost morale in your team meetings. As leaders, you surround yourself with overachievers and successful people. Ask them to join your team meeting and share their experiences. It shows recognition to your peers and brings new sources of inspiration and energy to your people.

Dorothy Boyd (26 year old single mom): 'In this age, optimism like that is a revolutionary act.'

Most sales teams tend to complain they are not listened to. Objectives are too high, the product has bugs, the roadmap is not visionnary enough...You name it. Encourage your team to share their struggles and objections, make a fair arbitrage of the complaints, work to address the important subjects with thorough follow-ups, and most importantly, provide regular updates and progress on how you are addressing the most impactful ones with other departments.

Jerry Maguire: 'I am out here for you. You don't know what it's like to be ME out here for YOU. It is an up-at-dawn, pride-swallowing siege that I will never fully tell you about, ok? Help me... help you. Help me, help you.'

Remotely, you may feel half blind so how do you avoid falling into the trap of micromanaging and becoming over demanding on reporting? Routine check-in and mandatory every morning team coffee was a best practice during the covid situation. But, in the long run, it defies the purpose of a well-oiled operating rhythm. Favor efficiency over control, avoid scheduling meetings at lunchtime or after 6 pm or on last-minute notice. People need their personal time to be respected.

Jerry Maguire: 'There is such a thing as manners, a way of treating people.'

Maintain key vital meetings such as team gathering, deal reviews, and favor accountability & execution in your communication. Favor short, actionable emails and structured follow-up and avoid the multiplication of channels (slack/email/drive...) in your transmissions.

Dorothy Boyd: 'Stop...just stop. You had me at hello.'

Don't forget that being a manager is about supporting your people in being their best of themselves. Educate them on the importance of open communication and transparency. Trust goes both ways. As always, a leader should lead by example: create open agendas and don't be scared to add your personal time, sports and family lunches in there.

Jesus of CopyMat: 'That's how you become great, man. Hang your balls out there!'

There was a time when you would travel many hours for one face-to-face meeting. During this time you used to talk to your teammates, debrief from the meetings, you would catch up on your colleagues' social and personal life. You might even have gone to lunch. These moments were valuable times to get to know each other and learn how to work more efficiently with one another. Making personal conversations creates intimacy, whether within the team or with a potential client, its value is priceless.

Transport time used to be a routine part of the salesperson's day. It was a time for self-reflection, admin catch-up, and email follow-up. Following the pandemic it was evident that a lot of face-to-face meetings could now be conducted remotely, increasing productivity drastically. Instead of the traditional two to three customer meetings a day, you can now pack your agenda with up to seven customer interactions.

Therefore, managers must fit in casual check-ins, non business-related talks. Make it an opportunity to ask about the family, the kids' school, or share cooking and fitness insights. Productivity is not about working non-stop behind a computer for eight hours. Many studies have proven the necessity to recharge through break time for physical activities, lunch with the family, and possibly, personal development. As a leader, recognizing these elements is crucial not only to your employees' well-being and their capacity to work efficiently. Why not organize a walking outside team meeting?

Jerry Maguire: 'But if anybody else wants to come with me, this moment will be the ground floor of something real and fun and inspiring and true in this godforsaken business and we will do it together!'

The 20s have been challenging, to say the least. Many B2B companies saw their sales and pipeline drop. Others have boomed. Companies worldwide have accelerated their digital presence to ensure their survival.

Prospecting[20] in times like this is a bit of why and a lot of who. Are you targeting the right companies at the right time? Are you mission-critical to the companies you are trying to reach? After all, inside sales and large territory salespeople have been doing it for decades. It is a matter of adjusting. Here are some best practices:

- select prospects to whom you will be a priority (annual report, strategy, press announcement)
- select personas and craft personalized messages, use social media to connect with prospects
- offer short meeting connections & virtual coffees

Social selling is the combination of creating a personal/professional brand of expertise online and leverage the capacity to network digitally by engaging with others (comments, likes, repost) and creating new relationship. As such, social selling is no longer a nice-to-have skill, the rules of social selling are ever moving and it can be overwhelming to get into it. However, it has definitely proved to be effective, efficient and valuable. In fact I had clients getting a 30%

---

[20] Refer to the end of the chapter for a social selling prospecting cadence in complex selling.

conversion on their social selling actions. In addition, sales (and the entire revenue team) should now more than ever, have a personal brand: what is their expertise, experience, what kind of value can they bring to the prospect? This should be part of your enablement path, make your people digitally popular for their expertise.

Many sales professionals are currently struggling with **creating intimacy and expanding their network**. If you have held a zoom meeting with five people, connect with them individually with a crafted message on Linkedin. Suggest a 15 minute phone call and casually meet. If you notice some people are invited to your presentation, do your best to connect with each of them individually and collect their expectations before the general meeting. If someone is copied in an email, understand why by connecting with them.

Jerry Maguire: 'All right, I'll tell you why you don't have your ten million dollars. Right now, you are a paycheck player. You play with your head, not your heart. In your personal life, heart. But when you get on the field it's all about what you didn't get. Who's to blame. Who won through the pass. Who's got the contract you don't. Who's not giving you your love. You know what, that is not what inspires people. That is not what inspires people! Shut up! Play the game, play it from your heart.'

Don't forget that a personal assistant is resourceful and can provide you with insights and even sometimes assistance in networking an account. Talking to one person is not enough. Do not fear asking for a warm introduction. Do not think you are losing time talking to lower people in the org chart.

Dicky: 'The key to this business is personal relationships.'

Adaptability is the key to success. As new ways become dominant, reinventing ways of doing business is key not only to your success but also, to your well-being.

Dicky Fox: 'Hey, I don't have all the answers. In life, to be honest, I failed as much as I have succeeded. But I love my wife. I love my life. And I wish you my kind of success.'

Plot summary

❖ Consider that the future of work is evolving constantly and requires adaptation.

❖ Favor quality over quantity, shorter meetings, personalized prospection, short 5 minutes connection with potential prospects.

Ready, set, action!

❖ Talk to your team, how do they feel, what are their needs, how do they adjust to increased productivity and remote working?

❖ Stay close to future of work studies, articles and recommendation, take into account best practicesmental health, stability and boundaries.

Cadence recommendation (to be adjusted to your business for complex selling outbound prospecting)					

S T A R T	W e e k 1	Identify 5 accounts in your ICP Identify 5 personas in each account Follow the personas on linkedin Digest the personas' linkedin activity Start account mapping (news, business strategies, interviews, ...) Check for warm introduction and partner leverage			
L E A R N	W e e k 2	Social selling engagement with personas Comment smart comments that differentiate and spark a conversation Create a social post with news from companies, digest their content, bring expertise in your text	Add step from week 1		
E X E C U T E	W e e k 3	Continue Social Selling Engagement If engagement -> add the persona on linkedin with personal note, engage conversation If no engagement -> send a personal email, hyperpersonalization eg. VITO letter (you can add a physical letter/package with whitepaper notes etc.) Use Lusha etc. for cold emails	Continue with new accounts step week 2	Add step from week 1	
I D E A L R U N	W e e k 4	Prepare for calling with all the warm up done in week 1-3 Use the social selling warm up to break the ice If there was no social selling interaction, use account knowledge to break the ice. Always bring value. Make it short (less than 30s) to book a meeting that has value for your prospect (not a demo!) Possible addition with: invite persona to be speaker at a Panel (physical event) invite persona to be speaker at a Panel/or guest at a Webinar invite persona to participate in a Blog interview for your website invite persona to participate to your company podcast channel (aka expertise, not product!) ...and so on	Continue with step week 3	Continue with new accounts step week 2	Add step from week 1
I D E A L R U N	W e e k 5	If you cannot get access to the persona, there is no contact, no engagement and you are have completed all the step in the process. Drop into nurturing (newsletter, invite to event), re engage if/when there is movement	Continue with step week 4	Continue with step week 3	Continue with new accounts step week 2

In week 4, 5 and next you have moved the full complex selling engine of 25 accounts, 100 personas with a personal outreach and value added, therefore maximizing chances of high value conversion, while boosting your personal brand digitally

THE ROLE OF THE CUSTOMER SUCCESS DEPARTMENT

Gomothered

This chapter highlights the revenue architecture's underdog, looking closely at what the customer success department does for your company, with a new spin on an old fashion fairytale. Let's find out if the customer success manager is the modern fairy godmother to your clients.

Agnes (Godmothered): 'Once upon a time, there was a magical place called the Motherland, where Fairy Godmothers lived and learned all they needed to know about godmothering. Oh, blah, blah, blah. We all know how this bit goes.'

In Saas organizations, the happily ever after can quickly become a nightmare to coordinate, especially the processes to put in place are supposed to guarantee the perennity of your future income. How do you set up a customer success department to ensure customer satisfaction, adoption, value, renewals, and growth?

Agnes: 'This is Moira, the headmistress. She wrote the book on Fairy Godmothering, literally. She's been banging on about the same old formula for centuries. Yesterday, we reviewed step one.'

The customer success department fosters long-term relationships with customers by reaching out to them proactively, contrary to customer support, who is responsive and reactive to customer issues. As their name implies, the customer success department ensures the client is experiencing measurable success with your company's solution. Meanwhile, the account manager focuses on growing the size of the client account by bringing additional revenue to the business.

The customer success department typically owns the renewal rate, NPS score, and churn rate. Some companies incentivize this department on additional revenue (upsell and or cross-sell) identification and collaboration.

As simple as it seems, this organization's success within your company depends tremendously on the foundation laid out for them from interactions before they take over by the sales and deployment team.

Mackenzie: "Life isn't as simple as happily ever after."

We have established that the customer success manager is not responsible for deploying the solution (unless it is a plug and play version), nor is it part of the support organization. Instead, they inherit customers who have invested money and, therefore, expect results. Any false promises made previously, such as fluffy return on investments or features not available in the platform, can be a source of frustrations which, untreated, could result in a crisis.

For this reason, your company must own the following ground rules:

Sales should not promise an impact on KPIs your solution does not have a direct effect on. Instead, identify the sub KPIs you can monitor and that your customer success will be able to use to build a KPI tree with an indirect impact on cost reduction, increased revenue and possibly, risk mitigation.

Mandate at least one executive who has the relationship history understands why the customer is investing and remains involved in quarterly business reviews after the implementation as reinsurance of leadership in the relationship and empowerment of the customer success department.

Prioritize accounts per revenue spent. It is only legitimate that the customers who spend the most get the best and most of your resources. The next in line is the clients representing the most significant potential: shared revenue roadmap and strong partnership (customers who are willing to invest in your solution and your future without changing your vision or product roadmap).

Last but not least, do not overlook the profiles of the people you recruit to manage the relationship with your top customers. A customer success manager is not a junior person. It is a consultant profile that understands the business strategies of large companies and can speak to an executive profile with confidence.

Eleanor: "I'm gonna prove that people still need fairy godmothers!"-

Your customer success managers should be capable of running KPI trees[21] with your customers. What is their current situation? What should they measure, and how? Most of your customers lack expertise in your innovative field. You must evangelize in every way, including showing them the course of which KPIs to choose from that are meaningful to their business and will monitor the success of your project. A predefined list of 20-30 sub-KPIs that are meaningful to the use case you will be addressing is a good way to ensure your customer feels comfortable picking at least five important and easy to measure.

Eleanor: "I came all this way to help you find your heart's desire!"

---

[21] Refer to the excellent book: KPI checklist by Bernie Smith

Once the ideal state is defined as well as the KPIs your customer will measure with your assistance, the customer success should put in place an operating rhythm of interactions including (but not limited to):

Bi-weekly: Scheduling meetings with the operational (and power users) to train them (new use cases, new features, how to boost adoption)

Regularly: Getting regular access to new people and team to evangelize your solution, the problems it solves, and the benefits and gain new supporters.

Monthly: Leadership (manager/director) sync up with a SWOT analysis of the project and KPIs dashboard.

Quarterly: Executive review with KPIs presentation, progress, SWOT analysis, and executive partnership (vision, roadmap, company updates...).

Last but not least we must explore the notion of customer satisfaction through testimonials. Customer stories are usually managed by the marketing department who is usually excellent at making things shiny and bright.

Which means, they will quote users (operational people) on how happy they are and avoid challenging the client on how they currently (or should) measure progress with meaningful KPIs. The problem is not how the marketing department does thing but how the entire operations work, because the people of marketing are rarely given access to the customer executives who understand the impact of your solution on their business.

Users testimonials are adapted for Product Led Growth companies building communities, it can also work well for transactionals selling but it diminishes the value in complex selling.

Sales and Customer Success Managers are responsible for successful and useful testimonials, they should prepare their customers, work their executive story with measurements and facilitate marketing access to their champions.

Before creating a testimonial ask your team:

- Is the person providing the testimonial at operational or business level?
- Are they willing to share the situation they were in before you fixed it in ways it highlights problems?
- Have you been helping them measure their success since using your solution with meaningful KPIs operational and business? Can they mention numbers in the interview?

Why is this important?

Customer testimonials are rare and valuable, simply because they can be leveraged in many forms: employee engagement, prospect validation, motivational kick off, public relations and lead attraction. You should use them to convince decision makers, budget owners, head of business units, CFOs, and C-levels in general.

Mackenzie: "People want to laugh and to hope and to see the magic in the world because it's real!"

Conclusively, to empower your customer success department:

1. Keep in mind that the churn is never their sole responsibility. Work the entire stream of the revenue architecture to understand the origin of the issues.

2. Support this department, the frontline of your customer satisfaction, the essence of your value to penetrate additional new business units, and identify new use cases to address.

Eleanor: "Forget ever after. Just live happily."

<u>Plot summary</u>

❖ CSMs have to understand how they can bring value quickly, set KPIs and metrics for how they will measure the success of the solution implementation.

❖ They have to create their own champions within the organization to obtain the commitment for resources and leadership support.

❖ It is better to be flexible and offer a reduction of the scope rather than have the customer churn completely. Consider this option when budget constraints are high and usage have decreased/are low.

<u>Ready, set, action!</u>

❖ In a moment of an economic downturn, their mission becomes impossible: what if the solution was never a priority to the management? What if no one at the prospect sees how they are attached to key strategic initiatives?

THE ART OF PARTING WAYS

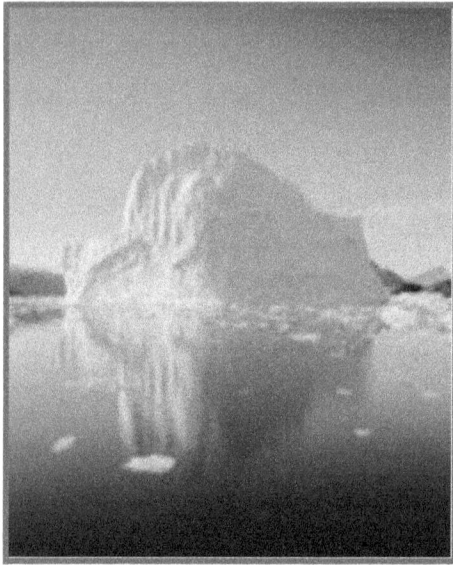

Titanic

Talking about separation is a tough conversation, to say the least. Parting ways is a burdensome task. For many leaders and entrepreneurs, it might even be the most draining one. Despite all the efforts you put into recruiting the right talents and putting the most adequate process in place; believing you can keep everybody safe, happy, creative, and efficient in the long run is as utopic as assuming *the Titanic* had no chance of sinking.

Cal: 'God himself could not sink this ship.'

Talents are usually best at a specific company stage. Rare are the entrepreneurs, executives and employees that can remain efficient and auspicious from early-stage to large-scale companies. Some are best at creative thinking, others are problem solvers while some excel at putting in place execution.

Some rare people are capable of doing it all, yet, you should not overlook the impact of their self-accomplishment, self-development, and ultimate happiness.

Rose DeWitt Bukater: 'It was the ship of dreams to everyone else. To me, it was a slave ship, taking me back to America in chains. Outwardly, I was everything a well brought up girl should be. Inside, I was screaming.'

Indeed, if talents are by definition comfortable with early stages, small environment startups, they may feel out of sorts as soon as the team grows, silos form, and a more 'rigid' structure is necessary. On the contrary, others are experts at the scale-up phase with larger teams, better resources, and processes already in place which they will improve and execute upon.

Rare are the people that can combine qualities and appetite for both roles and feel comfortable during the company's cultural changers. In fact, even independent board members have a limited time implication based on their 'stage' expertise and what they can bring to the table. This seems pretty logical, except when emotions, attachment, and pride come into play. Why is it then that when an employee, an executive or a founder is no longer finding satisfaction, contentment, and will, the relationship deteriorates drastically?

Rose DeWitt Bukater: 'I know what you must be thinking. "Poor little rich girl, what does she know about misery?"

Jack Dawson: 'No, no, that's not what I was thinking. What I was thinking was, what could've happened to this girl to make her think she had no way out?"

Why would you and your talents take a different path? Because of the unceasing evolution of the company, the most obvious reason is as stated above: the incapacity for some people to consistently adapt to arising changes, of letting go of doing it the 'old ways'. Old could be a three months to eighteen months time frame in the startup world. This is how fast the path is.

Similarly, the incapacity to rapidly acquire a new set of skills required to keep up with the organization may be a trigger. For the organization, providing the necessary means to catch up can represent a task too complex or cost consuming to handle. It does not mean that the person is not good enough, it does not mean this person is no longer a talent, it just means that they no longer are at the right place, at the right time.

Changes have consequences and are inevitable as you scale; their combination is often perceived as a drastic change of culture. This is a moment when the initial team does not have the room nor the resources for growth anymore. To support the company's thriving, new executives and new employees have to join, they bring their own experience, enabling more processes, setting up a new level of requirements. Sometimes, their arrival can be perceived as toxic. It happens that it quickly becomes a battle of the foundation team vs the scaling team.

There are several ways a separation can go:

The ones that do not want to leave.

Rose DeWitt Bukater: 'I'll never let go, Jack. I'll never let go.'

In this particular case, the attachment of the executive or employee is so strong that they will not consider leaving the adventure. They no longer fit, either because they cannot keep up with the constantly evolving new requirements and set of skills or simply because they remained into the early stages when everyone was important, heard and considered. It was a time when everyone could make a difference and receive recognition. When someone must go because it is no longer a fit but refuses to do so, it is one of the toughest decisions and actions to take. In this situation, remember to leave emotions and history aside. Unfortunately, even if that person is a pillar of likability when it is time to part, the best option is to do it before anyone gets hurt.

Older Rose: 'Can you exchange one life for another? A caterpillar turns into a butterfly. If a mindless insect can do it, why couldn't I?'

Not parting at the right time could lead to bad feelings, toxicity, and a possible strong impact on the overall team productivity if the person concerned was likable and had influence.

The ones you can't imagine doing without

Jack Dawson: 'Don't you do that, don't say your good-byes. Not yet, do you understand me?'

They have built your company, they are part of the foundation walls, they are the essence of your success, yet they have decided it is their time to abandon ship, join a new adventure. Because of all the efforts and sweat you have shared in building your company together, you cannot imagine doing without them and you are ready to reinvent everything in the company to keep their presence. This type of reaction is emotional. Do not go that route. When someone is ready to go, support them, keep them close, as an advisor, mentor, but do let them go. In fact, you'd be surprised, they may come back down the road with more experience and more will to kill it by your side.

The ones that are mature enough and make it smooth

Wallace Hartley: 'Gentlemen. It has been a privilege playing with you tonight.'

This is the easy-breezy piece of cake. In this case, both parties have a plan for this separation from the beginning. You have hired someone to do a certain job during a certain period of time, you both knew that after a few years and when the job would come to near completion it would be time to move on. This used to be the case of the chief digital officer, often hired to enable the digital transformation of large corporations, they knew their job would last for a determined period of time and this was the proof they had done their job well. In this type of situation, you have a mature, open discussion about what is best for the company moving forward including how to best organize the separation and transition.

The ones that should not have been

Last but not least there are cases of human errors. On paper, it should have been a perfect match, in reality, the talent transplant to your organization does not take. The new employee does not belong or is overwhelmed and within a few weeks, you feel responsible for hiring the wrong person but too guilty to engage in a clean separation. Don't. Freeing someone earlier than later is best not only for your organization but also for the person you are letting go of. Putting your talent under performance review and pressure to make it work is a cruel way to extend a situation you already know cannot work.

Rose DeWitt Bukater: 'Well, I'm fine...I'll be fine...really.'
Jack Dawson: 'Really? I don't think so. They've got you trapped, Rose. And you're gonna die if you don't break free. Maybe not right away because you're strong but...sooner or later that fire's gonna burn out...'
Rose DeWitt Bujater: 'It's up to you to save me, Jack.'
Jack Dawson: 'You're right...only you can do that.'

The important lesson is that not letting go at the right time, in the right manner can cost your company a lot. A toxic employee is contagious and will turn many others into demotivation, thus having a direct impact on productivity, revenue, and churn. Worst, your reputation will then precede you and make it difficult to hire true talents. To avoid this, discuss concerns with transparency, layout expectations and implications clearly, monitor and discuss the skill/will ratio on a regular basis (quarterly) with your talents.

As we end the chapter, you may ask yourself, how can I avoid a difficult breakup? The answer is simplicity and honesty: prepare for the break-up from the beginning. Lay out the foundations of your relationship from the start. Hire people that are aligned with this approach. Watch for the signs of overwhelmed emotions and toxicity and address them immediately. Accept that despite your efforts and preparation, there will be times when the termination remains heavy with sadness, incomprehension, and sometimes even anger.

No matter what, do not leave a situation as it is, take action as soon as you can in order to avoid sinking the culture and trustworthiness of your company.

Bruce Ismay: 'But this ship can't sink!'

Thomas Andrews: 'She's made of iron, sir! I assure you, she can. And she will. It is a mathematical certainty.'

Plot summary

- ❖ Avoiding the subject of separation is utopic.

- ❖ People will have to leave, people will go, you must learn to accept it to make the best of the situation.

- ❖ Rare are the people who can be efficient at all stages of a company life. Even if they can do it all, consider their happiness and satisfaction as their role evolves.

- ❖ Recruiting mistakes happen, it does not mean the person is not a talent. Cut it short to avoid toxicity and wasting both your time.

Ready, set, action!

- ❖ How do you react when you find out a recruit is not a fit? How long does it take?

- ❖ How often do you talk with the leadership team about their confidence in their role?

- ❖ How much do you engage in training your people to acquire new skills? Do you let your people learn their promotion job on the field?

BOOK III:

SALES PLAY

PROTECT YOUR LEADS FUNNEL

Forrest Gump

Who doesn't love a guy like Forrest Gump and his considerable life story? There are many lessons to learn from him and the most important is that he never thought any less of himself, no matter what.

"Stupid is as stupid does" is one of the most recurring quotes of the movie. This is the sentence Forrest uses to shield himself from the many attacks of his offenders. The meaning is powerful: what is the definition of stupid? People are not stupid, their behavior is. And

when it comes to lead management, attitude is everything.

"One day it started raining, and it didn't quit for four months. We been through every kind of rain there is. Little bitty stingin' rain... and big ol' fat rain. Rain that flew in sideways. And sometimes rain even seemed to come straight up from underneath. Shoot, it even rained at night..." – Forrest Gump

I like the idea of rain when it comes to <u>inbound</u> leads. Some people see the rain as a blessing, while others despise it. One thing is for sure, no matter where you live, there is no positive outcome to too much rain, and it is the same with too many inbound leads.

B2B Inbounds can be the most poisonous type of lead to your funnel because of this thing that is available to everyone now: the internet.

Nowadays, your prospect can find all the information they need before talking to a salesperson.

- Advice from peer buyers/users,
- Features and Functions comparison,

- Prices,
- Blogs and consulting advice from experts and more.

Your buyers may be part of communities, or they may have gotten incredible insights from one of the top consulting companies. In any case, at some point in time, they will have access to a well-furnished library of whitepapers, advice, and videos at hand and computer reach.

The tables have turned. A buyer, whether in the procurement function or a project manager, is informed and aware. When they knock on your door, their opinion is made.

This is the reason why, the natural reaction for many sellers is to, unfortunately, bend to the prospect's every wish.

*'Don't ever let anybody tell you they're better than you.' –
Mrs.Gump.*

But you shouldn't. Instead:

Align with your marketing team so that the Inbounds match your Ideal Customer Profile (ICP).

Apply a natural filter to the Inbounds before delivering them by priority order to your customer-facing team.

Smartly route the leads for you and your customer. If the Inbound is an existing customer, allocate directly (instead of through the SDR team) to the Account Management or Customer Success Management. If the Inbound matches an open opportunity, assign them to the corresponding Account Executive.

Train your lead management team to deal with Inbounds. Unlike the common assumption, Inbounds are not easy to work with. They should not be pitching your product first as an answer to the Inbound prospect's question, and please do not push them to book a demo without a proper discovery.

It is very easy for any SDR/BDR/AE to take the excitement of a prospect who wants to move forward quickly, pretend he has a budget, and that he is the decision owner. These inbounds can lead to nowhere or slip quarter to quarter if they are not heavily qualified: why are they doing the project? What problem are they solving? What initiatives and business strategies is it serving? Who in the organization is supporting this project (and How can we get access to them)?

When it comes to Inbound leads, the fewer, the better fare. Filtering ahead is essential to avoid overflowing your field teams. You want to choose quality over quantity.

As Forrest Gump would say, *'There's only so much fortune a man really needs, and the rest is just for showin' off.'*

Now, that is when your marketing machine is doing an outstanding job, or you've raised some extremely efficient attraction to the market.

When it comes to **Outbound lead management**, the theory and the best practices remain the same. As an unpopular opinion, I will just say that I do not believe in cold calling. I don't believe in classic prospecting in general. I am anti-cadences, anti-quantity, and unprepared calls. But... downright pro-activity!

Work hard, yes, but in a thoughtful way. Good prospecting is thoughtful prospecting that engages several pillars of the company with an actionable roadmap and an operating rhythm[22].

When you have a plan, the mind is free to be creative, and that's where the magic happens.

"Life is like a box of chocolates; you never know what you're gonna get." – Forrest Gump.

Enable targeting and specialization.

Let your SDRs and AEs choose a sector of activity to become the expert. In this way, they can have strategic conversations with their prospects. This way, the product subject is delayed until after they have positioned themselves as a trusted expert who understands their problems, anticipates them, and are able to solve them.

---

[22] Refer to the recommended prospecting cadence laid out at the end of chapter 'Managing Sales remotely'

Multiple entries

Lesser prospects to follow means your sales team can engage when their prospect is announced in a podcast, webinar, or article. They can listen, capture and use that material to make a connection. Public information is there to build relevant emails that speak to the prospect, even by including some of his own content in the title.

Engage socially and digitally.

- Has your team planned a demo? Take the list of speakers and propose 5 minutes of preparation to set up expectations. It avoids doing a long and uninteresting round table for the other speakers.

- Use Linkedin. Engage with your prospect, comment intelligent comments to make yourself known, be patient, and possibly engage in a conversation.

Bubba : 'Anyway, like I was sayin', shrimp is the fruit of the sea. You can barbecue it, boil it, broil it, bake it, saute it. Dey's uh, shrimp-kabobs, shrimp creole, shrimp gumbo. Pan fried, deep fried, stir-fried.'

Be creative, give it your best, don't let your people send average copy-pasted emails, and don't let them call without a purpose.

Forrest Gump 'You have to do the best with what God gave you.'

Advice to the leadership team: compensation plan, targets, OKRs and measurement will impact positively or negatively how your teams operate. Set the right objective to ensure shor- term qualification and long-term sustainable revenue.

Plot summary

❖ Both Inbound and Outbound require quality over quantity to have a high conversion rate

❖ Inbound leads require as much if not more qualification than outbound leads

❖ Inbound leads can grow your fake pipeline

❖ Routing of leads per ICP priority is important

❖ Train your people in having high level expertise qualification conversation

❖ Inbound leads are dangerous because the prospect has more information than you do

Ready, set, action!

❖ How do you consider a lead an opportunity? How many people do your sales team talk to per opportunity?

❖ How do you qualify inbounds? How much preparation do you give to Inbound lead qualification ahead of a call?

THE ART AND SCIENCE OF QUALIFYING

Sherlock Holmes

What do prospects want the most? They want you to make their time worthwhile. They need a return on time invested before even thinking about return on investment.

Therefore, it can appear better to investigate in advance to identify a potential fire and save everyone's time rather than jumping straight into the Oompa Lumpa song[23] of demos, POCs, and more. Now who would be better at investigating and deliberating such information than the famous or infamous Sherlock Holmes?

First things first, let's set the record straight. Qualifying is not about the BANT methodology, in which anyone must ask from the first call if the prospect has budget, authority, needs and timeline. Yet again, I am losing my mind over well-funded, established, and striving companies implementing BANT with, in fact, the most junior population of all: SDRs and BDRs.

'When we have inbounds, we must qualify more.' On that, we definitely agree! Does it mean you have to be rude? Because that's what BANT is, plainly rude and far away from a trusted advisor approach.

Let's just imagine you are on a date. You asked that person out (aka you are the inbound lead here).

---

[23] Oompa Lumpa from Charlie and the Chocolate Factory

During the appetizers, your date will start questioning your budget: Does your job pay well? Can you pay your rent? How much is your rent? Are you still somewhat sponsored by your parents? Do you have savings? Can you pay for this meal and all others?

During the main course, your date will move forward with asking you if you need any authorization from any third party to continue with the evening at another place of choice.

Before dessert, your date will then ask about the need: Why did you ask for a date? Why are you not in a relationship yet? Are you looking for something serious?

Finally, when the check comes, you might feel a bit exhausted, a bit frustrated, and somehow not listened to.

In essence, you absolutely did not connect with the person in front of you. Yet, this person will conclude that the answers are satisfactory and will pressure you in moving forward with the relationship by asking the Timeline you are setting yourself to get married and have children.

Logical?

Instead: Get into a conversation with your prospect and lead them to figure out that they have a problem(s) that needs fixing (not what they want to see, not what they want to improve, but what they want to fix). No problem = you are dealing with a 'see-more' who will check out all the right boxes of BANT by lying to you to get a demo, POC and more technical giveaway.

The best salespeople know that to become a trusted advisor, you must forget about telling them about your product and focus on understanding why they require it.

Dr. John Watson: 'What could she possibly need?'
Sherlock Holmes: 'It doesn't matter.'
Dr. John Watson: 'An alibi? A beard? A human canoe. She could sit on your back and paddle you up the Thames.'

Many startups and scale-ups believe they should close a deal as soon as a budget is agreed upon. When you provide a SaaS solution that requires enablement, education, and implementation, know that 100K is not just an annual contract value target. It is a minimum value that will get you the proper attention to secure resources on the customer side and avoid churn, it is also the necessary budget for a sales cycle of four months minimum and the capacity to reinvest in R&D. Unfortunately, it is often easier to secure a 30-40K budget and do transactional selling rather than building out the total value of your solution.

I talk to many sellers and companies, and to grasp a sales opportunity, my first question is (always): what's the pain?

And I often get an answer like:
They want to <u>increase</u>, they have to <u>improve</u>, they need a <u>better</u> solution...
Better, Faster, Stronger, More Efficient. All of these are nice to have. None of these are pains. And here is why: a pain is a problem.

Asking 'why' is the magic word for sales, only you cannot ask it in every sentence, you must use it wisely.

What is motivating the will to increase, to improve, to have 'better efficiency'? What happens if they don't do it? What are the negative consequences?

What would you reallocate your vacation budget for? Because that's what it is for your prospect, reallocating a budget that was not planned to fix an issue.

This is why, when you look at your opportunity you must remember that a pain is rooted in 'negative' statements such as I cannot do x, our market share is dropping, costs are piling up, and efficiency is affecting our capacity to deliver time to market.

Now, let's just imagine the case of a washing machine. We are four living at home and are all doing our fair share of sport. What would happen if our washing machine broke?

Would I buy a new one right away? Would I buy a premium one to avoid a cheap one breaking again in a month? Would I ask for additional services to have someone install it in the middle of the week?

Sherlock Holmes: 'My mind rebels at stagnation! Give me problems! Give me work!'

At the origin of it all is discovering a reason to act and ultimately unlocking the purchase. In sales books and methodologies, authors commonly refer to it as technical or functional pain. It is a capacity that is missing, something that your prospect cannot do without. E.g. Incapacity to automate, inability to analyze the data, inefficiency in the process...

If you stop at that, you may imagine the rest of the sentence, thinking, assuming these inabilities represent a big issue for your prospect. Unfortunately, what you assume is not always how it is.

Sherlock Holmes : [to Watson] 'Never theorize before you have data. Invariably, you end up twisting facts to suit theories instead of theories to suit facts.'

Therefore, never assume. Always confirm. Engage your prospect through an open, guided conversation. Use your empathy and likable personality. Draw your interlocutor into telling you about the 'horror' story of their technical issue. If you manage to get there, your prospect will come to realize the consequences of their inabilities. To avoid the horror stories happening repeatedly, your prospects must find a solution.

Sherlock Holmes : [Frenetically desiring more relevant information on the case] 'Data, data, data! I cannot make bricks without clay!'

A technical pain can generate interest in the prospects and secure the involvement of more stakeholders, especially if the team you are engaging with is the one suffering from it. Yet, if you stop just there in your investigation, the perimeter of your solution may never attract the attention of the executives, let alone their support and money.

Sherlock Holmes: 'Case reopened.'

You must understand the impact of the technical pain -and the horror stories- on the company's business. What are the consequences of this technical pain to the business? Are they losing market share to their competitors because they are not digitizing fast enough? Are they losing their talents because of repetitive manual tasks? Are they piling up costs at the customer call center because they are not providing a seamless customer experience? Why are these technical pains issues? To Whom? What are they doing to fix it? And what are the other initiatives put in place (that you can relate to)?

You must find out the consequences of the technical pains, for when the business is hurting, and the business understands why then budgets are found.

Sherlock Holmes: 'My journey took me somewhat further down the rabbit hole than I intended, and though I dirtied my fluffy whitetail, I have emerged, enlightened.'

When the business is suffering, influential people will take a personal interest in solving the matter to impact their career and future success. And when influential people take a troublesome issue under their responsibility, urgency appears.

Find the technical/functional pain, its impact on the team, the business, and the person who wants to fix it. Only then can you make sure they understand how you are the best partner and solution to their problems.

Proper qualification is the essence of a long-term customer/vendor relationship and the core of any successful sales organization. At the heart of it all is a good mix of artful skills, preparation, and good-natured curiosity combined with a brilliant mind to put it all together. Last, but not least, the art of qualifying relies in the capacity to identify when you must qualify out. There will be times when your prospect is simply not a match, the moment when you cannot solve their problems better than anyone else. Accept it. Move on. Convert the next one.

Sherlock Holmes: There was never any magic. Merely conjuring tricks.

Plot summary
- ❖ Qualification should not be synonym for interrogation, it requires art, preparation, empathy and curiosity
- ❖ There is more than one level of pain in a deal, just like there is more than one pain. There are differences between, operational and business impacts.
- ❖ Business impacts often unlock influential people, personally motivated to fix them

<u>Ready, set, action!</u>

- ❖ Create a set of engaging, TED (tell me, explain to me, describe to me) questions.

- ❖ Prepare your meeting by leveraging ice breakers: what does the company do? what are they trying to achieve? You should know as much as possible before meeting with them.

- ❖ Spend time in qualification, not many meetings but the good part of a meeting. Don't pitch, listen, engage and dig

ASSUMPTIONS, OBJECTIONS &
NEGOTIATIONS

Red notice

Are Assumptions, Objections, and negotiations[24] worth a Red Notice?

What else than the three most wanted subjects - assumptions, objections, and negotiations- in complex selling to match Netflix's greatest blockbuster yet,

---

[24] For a dedicated chapter on Negotiation, refer to Popcorn to the new CEO, Negotiations with Jack Sparrow and Negotiating with giants, Peter D Johnston

mainly when it includes the witty, punchy, and humorous trio that is Dwayne Johnson, Gal Gadot and Ryan Reynolds? Let's explore what we can learn from them in strategizing and planning our prospect reactions.

Assumptions

Whether you are in business development (SDRs, BDRs), in sales (AEs, AMs), in presales (SCs, SEs), or even in Customer Success (CSMs), there will be a time when you must know precisely what happens to your prospect in a level of depth you may have considered unnecessary.

The one thing that can prevent you from making a deep discovery is not the stage of the opportunity, your role, or the prospect's reluctance to open up.

The one thing that can prevent you from making a deep discovery is yourself and making assumptions.

After all, Ryan Reynolds, aka Booth in Red Notice, assumes Agent John Hartly is a noble agent from the Federal Bureau of Investigation. But is he? And by making this assumption, is he taking a more challenging route than he should have?

When you present a lead, an opportunity, an upsell or a cross-sell to your team, prepare the following non exhaustive list of questions:

- Why is this important to my prospect?
- Why are they looking to achieve this goal?
- What happens if the prospect does not deliver on his strategy?
- Who says they are not doing enough/not efficient enough/not fast enough? Who is giving the mandate to fix it?
- Why is the situation presented by my prospect a problem to them, and what other initiatives are they putting in place to fix it?

As Inspector Das would say: "What can I say? I like to be thorough."

Now, if at any point in time, your manager or your team asks you or you ask yourself any of these questions, and you feel like answering with 'I think,' 'I believe,' or 'most likely because.' Stop. Right. There.

I know, and you know the customer did not give you these insights. You are coming up with what you *think* might be the correct answer. But no one told you because you did not ask, and you cannot accept saying 'I don't know,' so you come up with an 'I think' made-up answer.

Nolan Booth: "You sneaky little minx. Where'd you learn that? Profiler school?"

Assumptions are leaving behind key insights to move forward. Often, they are the symptom of someone who talks more than he/she listens. The question is, how did you get there? At the company level, I blame too much product love. You read that right. Too much training on the product, customer stories, or use cases training leads your revenue team to act like they know it all. You have to train them to listen. Much like a psychologist can deduce the patient's issue, it does not mean they have to prescribe anything without going to the bottom of the issue. The customer story is your most powerful asset.

Nolan Booth: "For all I know, you could be the bad guy, and I could be the other bad guy."

Now, nobody is blaming anybody here. We are all learning. If you are a manager, enable your people to go back and gather insights. Only then can you help them formulate questions and understand your prospect's situation; this is valuable at any point in time in a vendor/prospect/customer relationship, even in an advanced relationship/sales process.

- What you think is a problem might not be one for your customer.
- What you believe someone will do (or think) may not happen.
- Who you think has power and influence may be your detractor.
- What process you feel you might have to check can be/or become exceptionally more complex.

And so on...

So, well, as Booth would say: "If You Don't Know That, Then You Really Are Dumber Than I Look."

Objections

It goes without saying- the more you go into assumptions mode, the more your customer/prospect will feel disconnected from you and your company. As you build distance by lack of genuine interest, objections will arise. Rest assured, all good sales campaigns come with objections, regardless of your company's listening skills.

The main question is whether the objection is emotional or rational. Depending on its origins, you will not treat these objections in the same way.

An emotional objection is linked to an emotion or a fear, which must be welcomed and understood. Here are some examples:

'It's too expensive' might mean: I am not responsible for this kind of budget and I am feeling **uncomfortable** justifying this amount.

'I'm too busy' might mean: I'm not responsible for the subject, and I am not sure who might be or I do not want to **assume** anything.

'I don't need' might mean: I'm **frustrated** with your approach and I'm not attached to your product pitch.

Booth: "I Was Going To Carry You In My Heart Like An Eternal Flame, You Stupid Complainer."

To be treated correctly, an emotional objection must welcome the emotion with empathy and understand its root before even considering how to defuse the objection. In all cases, you must avoid any type of defense. It is absolutely necessary to greet the emotion without judgment and as always, ask questions in a non interrogative manner by making them feel at ease. With more information, you can build a new game plan.

Side note: 'Ghosting' can be a form of Objection with many emotions associated with it. For the one who is ghosted: frustration, anger, incomprehension, and sometimes even panic when the quarter/number/job is at stake.

Inspector Das: "Now, normally, I'm not a vindictive person, but, well, I trusted you and you hurt my feelings."

For the one who is ghosting: shame. A person who wants to work with you actively and who suddenly ghost you is most likely ashamed. They do not know how to tell you that they could not get the budget or the necessary approval.

Do not shame ghosters. Instead, find a way to help them feel comfortable sharing their vulnerability, re-engage with them, and start the communication by being extra understanding by opening a safe zone such as 'it's ok if the deal went south, let's talk about it'.

Hartley: 'See? I'm A Good Guy... But Sometimes I Do Bad Things.'

Not all re-engagement will save the business opportunity. Still, at a minimum, it will save the great relationship you have built with your prospect and maybe a future champion in life.

Now, the best objections are rational objections that are based on reliable information.

'I found more expertise elsewhere' is a fact that is backed up with data, therefore rational.

'There are many options (competitors) out there' means they are trying to figure out how you differentiate.

Rational objections are a blessing if you know how to handle them. The person is actually opening up. But before trying to defend your position, you must take the opportunity to explore with open questions, 'tell me about the expertise you need...' to find the best strategy and find a path to diffuse the objection.

Bishop: 'I Want You To Remember One Critically Important Thing: I Know Everyone You Work With And Every Member of Your Family. And I Also Know Your Browser History.'

An emotional objection lacks urgency and necessity -it's a response to a problem. In contrast, the rational objection has already considered the problem but is not convinced that you are the best solution -yet).

Now that we have covered the necessity to gather as much information as possible in the process, we can use it in the process of **negotiation**. Underlying the balance of a win-win deal for your company lies the necessity to protect yourself, your employees, and your reputation. You take the responsibility to put your people first before the money and that means you have the power to walk away.

If you have done your job right, you have uncovered issues you can fix better than anybody else and you have developed champions. You have built your value because you are the experts who can support the prospect/client's priorities if, after all that (not just the one interview), you find yourself in a discouraging position. Then, be ready to walk away.

Discouraging here could mean that the giant you are negotiating with can be asking too much from you, free stuff, discounts, new pricing, resources that you cannot afford, and contracts that are twisting your arm.

Hartley: "We're Not Partners. This Is A Marriage of Convenience."

This is your moment. Walk away. While remaining professional, try to bring out their empathy:

You have the following problem {X}, we can solve it with our solution {unique differentiators Y}.

We invest in our R&D to always serve you better than others (expertise, vision).

We understand that you do not currently have the budget to move forward.

However, we cannot align with the substantial discount you are looking for.

At this stage, to fit into your budget would mean:

- putting you at risk of not providing you with the best service
- putting the sustainability of our company at risk (if I do this with you, I have to do it with others).

It may not be the right timing for us to work together, but the elements may change in the future. Let's stay close and in touch.

Hartley: 'There Are Two Bishops In Chess.'
Bishop: 'And A Whole Lotta Pawns.'

Use them all, but do not sacrifice your people.

Bishop: 'You Can Have Excuses Or Results, Not Both.'

Plot summary
- ❖ Assumptions are common when we can tell the rest of the story on behalf of our customer. too much product training and customer success stories can lead to revenue team assuming
- ❖ Objections have two types Emotional and Rational, they are not treated in the same way
- ❖ The power of negotiations lie in the discovery, the understanding of the problem and our capacity to build value by solving the problem. Information is power in negotiation so is the capacity to walk away.

<u>Ready, set, action!</u>

- ❖ How often do you respond with 'I think', 'I believe' when you have to tell your customer story?

- ❖ Have you ever made a difference between emotional and rational objections?

- ❖ How much information do you own, how confident are you about the pain and solution story before entering negotiation?

STORYTELLING & REVENUE

The never ending story[25]

Building lasting and robust revenue should come from a strong foundation with your customer. They are making an investment in your vision, based on a common understanding shared at the highest executive level. You are committing to take your customers further than any of their traditional vendors. To do that, you must look further than the product, beyond the solution, and harness the beauty of the storytelling to craft a *never-ending story* with your clients.

---

[25] Photo from Nong Vang on Unplash

Storytelling is not just an art. When you base your story on properly qualified facts gathered through detailed workshops, it can become an absolute masterpiece. However, if you've never done this before, you will probably face the infamous writer's block: where should I start?

Bastian: 'Why is it so dark?'
The Childlike Empress: 'In the beginning, it is always dark.'

Accept that the product does not do it all.

Having a stellar product and being the leader in your market can hold back your current and future revenue architecture.

Wait what?

Overconfidence in the product creates what I call the balance default: you've put all your eggs in one basket. The product is excellent. It almost 'sells itself.'

So why hire senior people? Why invest in your SDRs when they can be calling machines? Why not focus on quantity? It does not matter if the demos are unprepared as long as you are doing tons of them. This attitude forces - at best- your Account Executives and pre-sales to deliver demos quickly without understanding the prospect <u>story</u>. Therefore, to ensure the prospect's investment they push a <u>standard</u> business case made of fictitious Return On Investment (ROI) that remains a <u>feeble</u> promise on the procurement desk or CFO.

Because of the volume of leads, your sales people will put themselves into transactional selling mode and your average sales price (and Average Recurring Revenue -ARR) will rarely pass the bar of a 100K deal. The product is a shining star. but at a lower value.

In value selling, selling too low puts your Customer success department in a position where they have to fight to maintain and build long-term relationships and avoid the churn. You have great people in your team, people who want to create value but do not dare to go through a thorough qualification process because of the pressure of expectation from the company sales process.

The Childlike Empress: 'Bastian. Why don't you do what you dream, Bastian?'

Bastian: 'But I can't, I have to keep my feet on the ground!'

Believe that people buy from people.

To avoid such a scenario, one doesn't necessarily have to hire a seasoned sales team. Building strong, sustainable revenue streams requires relying on partnerships: customers who have perceived your solution's value from the early days and prospects who share the dream at an executive level. Taking the time to lay out the foundation for these powerful, lasting relationships will secure exponential revenue. Relationships form over trust. A bond that anyone in a customer-facing role (SDR, AE, AM, CSM etc.) must cherish and gain by:

- being a natural at understanding the issues the solution should solve,
- summarizing the ideal solution,
- reformulating their interlocutors' expectations with the prospects words.

Being a trusted advisor and focusing on value selling enables the customer-facing person to uncover and develop future champions who will carry your company's flagship to their executives.

Falkor: 'Having a luck dragon with you is the only way to go on a quest.'

Co-create a powerful business story

By now that you have grasped the importance of qualification and building champions. Before sending any numbers and proposals, sit down with your prospect to write the story together, it is an executive briefing, no longer than a page, a narrative commonly known as the three whys: why should the prospect do the project, why should they do it with you, why now?

Why should the customer do the project?

Often, when your product is only perceived as a benefit, you may end up being a nice to have rather than a priority. Do not put yourself at risk. This section is your opportunity to avoid the biggest competitor of all : the 'do nothing', the void, the status quo.

Atreyu: 'What is the Nothing?'

G'mork: 'It's the emptiness that's left. It's like a despair, destroying this world. And I have been trying to help it.'
Atreyu: 'But why?'
G'mork: 'Because people who have no hopes are easy to control; and whoever has the control... has the power!'

This part of the executive summary should be a condensed understanding, in your prospect's words, of the things they cannot do: the technical issues and their functional and business impact. If you were able to quantify the impact, even better, add it in here. Start by laying out your understanding of their corporate objective, how they want to achieve it with business strategies, the initiatives that are in place but at risk due to the operation problems, insert yourself into their company story. Work the story with your champion.

Why should the customer do it with you?

If you have implicated real issues that need fixing, then you've done the most challenging job of all. Nevertheless, it is important for your own sake to attach the highest issue (criticality) to your solution. Here, in your champion/customer's own words, tell the story of why they chose your solution over anything else. Don't stop at the obvious features/functions that solve the technical problems. Add your holistic differentiators: who you are, who your investors, your customers, where your vision comes from, and the boundaries will disappear.

G'mork: 'Fantasia has no boundaries.'
Atreyu: 'That's not true! You're lying.'
G'mork: 'Foolish boy. Don't you know anything about Fantasia? It's the world of human fantasy. Every part, every creature of it, is a piece of the dreams and hopes of mankind. Therefore, it has no boundaries.'

Lock it in with a true compelling event; why do it now?

If you struggle to find an answer here, it is most likely because you could not implicate a business impact. Think about it, every week that passes, the business impact piles up, your compelling event is right there: losing talents, losing market share, revenue at risk, reputation at stake... Just make sure your customer not only has a good understanding of the implications but is willing to act on it.

Storytelling is an art, and finding the right content is a science. When you work hand in hand with your customer to create strong foundations, the revenue will flow and remain, taking your valuation to whatever you want it to be.

Bastian's Father: 'I got a call from your math teacher, yesterday. She says that you were drawing horses in your math book.'

Bastian: 'Unicorns. They were unicorns.'

3 WHY: Best practices & structure template

The 3 why is an executive one pager, a narrative that your deal champion can bring to the executive buyer to get his buy in. It must be understandable by a financial person. Use only an executive language.

Remember the notion of narrative : you are writing a story, something that cannot be delivered in bullet point, a story that will be carried by your Deal

Champion[26] to the Economic Buyer[27].

Why do anything?

Start with a strong opening Corporate Objective/goal[28]:

What is the company's corporate objective? What is their business and financial goal? Eg: revenue target, specific online revenue, digital growth, reducing cost drastically, or, protecting their reputation as they are exploring the digital world...

Eg: "Company is growing at an exponential rate, with a target growth of 25% year on year."

Continue with the business strategies and initiatives :

What are the business strategies they are putting in place to support the corporate objective and goal?

---

[26] The person who understands the value of your solution to fix their problems and can present it in positive business impact to the leadership.

[27] The person who, if they say yes, no one else in the company can go against the purchase of your solution.

[28] Refer to the corporate objectives chapter and Value Pyramid template, ideally you must have a value pyramid by the time you create this exec briefing.

Eg: 'Open a new market, acquire another solution, invest in research and development to expand our portfolio...'

Finish with your understanding of what is preventing them from achieving their initiatives. What are there challenges (pains, problems) and how it is affecting them.

Use the information from your discoveries to layout the functional pains and their business impact in a way that is understandable and digestible by a financial, executive person.

Eg: 'However, we have no visibility on this new region to take actionable decisions./ We are struggling in engaging the people from our new acquisition./We are lacking developers to accelerate in our research and development.'

Why do it with -your company-?

Continue with presenting the assessment of the market, followed by your differentiators (unique, comparative, hollistics) presented in a neutral format.

After careful analysis of the market, we have decided that xxx is the most appropriate partner to support this endeavor. Our decision is based on the following criteria:

eg: capacity to enable our team with immediate insights on the region we are targeting within digestible dashboards / capacity to engage new employees in our legacy culture and on board them effectively/ capacity to automatically screen, select and engage with candidates to boost our developers team.

Select and develop the required capabilities that will be relevant at the leadership and executive level.

Why now?

Urgency and compelling event : What is the impact of waiting? What are the negative consequences on the business? Use the business pain and the impact of doing nothing. Each wee that passes should put your prospect at risk for revenue loss, cost increase or reputation impact.

Plot summary

- ❖ Storytelling is an art that requires practice, the science is how you build the content.
- ❖ Why your customer should do the project should attach to their company business strategies.
- ❖ Why your customer should do it now depends on the implication of the business pain.

Ready, set, action!

- ❖ Build the story in three part, why do it, why do it with you, why do it now
- ❖ Fill the gap with you champion(s)
- ❖ Avoid talking in nice to have (better, faster, strong, increase...) words

BUSINESS CASE & ROI

Hocus Pocus[29]

Whether you are a fan or not of the Halloween season, building a business case to prove return on investment in a sales campaign is just: a bunch of Hocus Pocus. Many scale-ups have learned and developed a sales process with critical stages, one of which is often: proving the ROI.

---

[29] Photo by Taylor Rooney on Unsplash

Jenny: 'How much candy have you had, honey?'

Of course, Return on Investment is essential to anyone spending money, especially when the budget is an annual recurring spend.

Winifred Sanderson: 'Oh, cheese and crust! He's lost his head! Damn that Thackery Binx!'

Knowing the pain story is essential to avoid running toward a poor ROI, no matter how good the metrics are, productivity alone is a good example of poor ROI.

Ask yourself: is improving productivity enough to make a customer invest in your solution?

If your solution can reduce 80% of someone's time (and salary?) by automating some low-value added task, you may think you have found the business pain. It is rarely the case, companies and CFOs do not invest to make someone's day job easier or less painful (unfortunately) they invest because the solution will fix something bigger.

Say that person (or team) is supposed to deliver a product, and they miss their time to market...In this particular case, a competitor can sweep a good percentage of market share away.

Say that person (or team) is supposed to provide key data analysis to executives to make strategic decisions but is only delivering partial information or mistaken information due to lack of time or human errors...The executive can take a wrong direction putting the company at risk.

Say that person (or team) is supposed to prevent outages, but the only way they can do it is by treating the information manually, and they are overwhelmed (and overworked)...The outages pile up, and customers leave to another provider.

Do not stop at 'just' productivity. Get the 'horror' story... What are the consequences? What has happened in the past? Paint the picture for them: it could happen if you do not act now to prevent it. You must attach to a bigger problem for the CFO to invest in your solution.

Remember that software vendors have been pushing ROI to their prospects without context for decades, you do not want to be another one of them.

Max: 'Fine, but everyone here knows that Halloween was invented by the candy companies. It's a conspiracy.'

Building a business case with your customer once you have the entire pain story can be powerful if the prospects comply with all of the three conditions listed below:

1. He has been **asking** for a business case-> you are not offering it without an ask.
2. He is actively **sponsoring** the process-> he needs it, and you will find out why.
3. He is **transparent** on why you need to do it and how to be the most accurate -> sharing of metrics and open discussion in individual interviews.

Unfortunately, this lineup of conditions is rarely adequately respected. Therefore, sales organizations tend to put themselves in a risky situation:

1. The ROI method has been known by procurement and CFOs for decades as a vendor method to obtain a budget. They will not fall for fluffy, made-up numbers, no matter how good they look.

2. You cannot ever guarantee an ROI. It depends on the customer's commitment to making it work, from resources to processes. The technology alone never does wonder just by itself. There are always people behind, making and taking decisions, even in IT.

3. The ROI you manage to calculate could be way below your perceived value for the prospect. If you are solving a significant pain with a rational and emotional impact, the reason to act is vital at a premium.

Sarah Sanderson: "This is...this is terribly uncomfortable."

Now, everyone who has incorporated an ROI phase in their sales process will ask the obvious: what do you recommend doing instead?

Master's Wife: 'Aren't you broads a little bit old to be trick or treating?'

1. Focus on the value you can bring to the table (not features!)

2. Focus on building your executive briefing value-case with your champion(s)

3. Make sure it is presented to the highest level in a digestible CFO readable format: attach yourself to their business strategies, become a priority: if they do not solve their technical problems with your solution, they cannot deliver on the committed business strategies.

Then, you want to build up a strong case of metrics for your prospect to measure the benefits of your solution and therefore upsell/cross-sell and avoid churn.

The customer success team should define- before implementation- a ground zero/foundation situation. What are the most important KPIs to the customer? Are they shared by the entire team of executives? Are they interested in these KPIs, and why? What do you want to have an impact on? List a long list of meaningful KPIs with the newly signed client, then figure out what you can measure to get started.

Commit your customer to monitor the KPIs weekly/bi-weekly/ monthly, and quarterly and regularly follow up with key stakeholders. If the performance is there, you have proven ROI and renewal, upsell and cross-sell budget. If the performance is not where it should be, you can identify the issues and fix them. They can lie in your own technology or be the customer's responsibility. This is the opportunity to call the customer's executive for attention and help on adoption, commitment, and resources to make it work.

Bus Driver: 'Bubble, bubble. I'm in trouble!'

This is a virtuous circle for your company. As you start monitoring meaningful KPIs with your customers and building dashboards to prove the performance and optimization, everyone becomes more confident. Renewals flow, customers willingly engage in additional budget spending, and your sales organization can leverage these metrics to add expertise and value to your new prospects.

Winifred Sanderson: 'I put a spell on you and now you're mine.'

Plot summary

❖ A ROI approach without identified issues, it's like eating chocolate after washing your teeth: it's useless!!

❖ If your client is not in pain, a good ROI is something he will consider from afar, if at all.

❖ If you make the ROI, it's your language, your way of doing things, your math, your metrics, your stats, what impact will that have on a CFO?

❖ In summary, yes to the business case if it is co-created with your client after working together on the solution he needs to solve his problems = real long-term partnership with high added value.

Ready, set, action!

❖ Look at the deal, why is an ROI important —
    is it because the customer needs it in his
    buying process or...have you you fell into the
    trap of imposing a ROI.

❖ Ask how your prospect is typically justifying
    investments (to the CFO, to the Board, etc).

❖ Ask how they usually proceed, do they build a
    business and if so, get to know how in an
    advanced level of details to best participate in
    their business case process.

THE DECISION MAKER

The Invisible Man

Once upon a time, I used to be a sales representative myself. In that life I built Champions at the CIO and CRO level. It is a pleasure to continue the relationship with a handful of them. This chapter is, like any other, inspired from real field experience but it is more in the sense it is the extract of the conversation I had during a lunch with the CTO of a large group.

His perspective on sellers is not only stimulating, it is a glimpse into how the smaller and bigger companies buy out there. I was always going to keep his anonymity to take it one step further, I'll make him the Invisible Man.

The Invisible Man : [talking to himself] 'There's a way back. God knows there's a way back! If only they'd leave me alone.'

We started our lunch talking about my latest article about revenue architecture, and his feedback threw me back in my seat.

'Caroline, even the most established and public companies do not know what they are doing. Most customer success managers are too technical, too junior, or too scared to call me. Last week, I sat in a meeting with a customer success manager who had been repeating over and over again the word 'crisis' within less than three sentences.'

'Were you in a crisis?' I asked.

'Not at all,' he laughed. But I had to scream high to the number two of the company because I could not get the attention I needed nor deserved without screaming', he winked.

'So what happened?'

'Well, I asked her why she had mentioned the word crisis five times and what was the crisis about. She told me someone had said I was unsatisfied. So I asked her our favorite question.'

And both said 'why?', smiling.

Of course, the poor lady had no clue, no one had told her, because no one, even her boss, had asked what was wrong. And, unfortunately, she had not dared asking the CTO. The customer success manager had not called him once since the deal was signed. Was it her fault? Obviously not. She was probably too scared to 'call high', not empowered to do so, or maybe even blocked by the account manager (sales rep) who had moved on to other deals to close.

The Invisible Man : [in an oily, menacing voice] 'There is no need to be afraid, Kemp. We are partners.'

Even if you believe you have more solution stickiness because of a significant investment - people and money-from a top customer, your short term reputation is at risk when you drop the ball after a deal. I often say, think about your customer experience and the consequences of anything else but state of the art delivery.

My former champion was complaining, so I had to challenge him. 'You're not the easiest person to have access to. You make it difficult on top of that. Imagine all those SDRs who are mandated to make endless calls to C-levels.'

He laughed. Not a chance they'd get a meeting with him, not with automated emails cadences and a lack of personalization. Was it really his fault? Shouldn't he be cautious of protecting his most valuable asset: his time?

The Invisible Man: 'All right, you fools. You've brought it on yourselves! Everything would have come right if you'd only left me alone. You've driven me near madness with your peering through the keyholes and gaping through the curtains, and now you'll suffer for it!'

My anonymous CTO continued, teasing: 'I have nothing against the salespeople; but can't they do a bit of the work? Most sellers come to our meetings empty-handed, without preparation. This annoys me the most. Don't you teach people how to know my business strategies and issues before meeting me?'

The Invisible Man: 'One day, I'll tell you everything. There's no time now.'

I cleared my throat. 'Yes, as a matter of fact, I personally do and care about it deeply. But not all companies teach their sales representative how to properly prepare and, even when they do, not all the salespeople care enough to take the time and do it thoroughly.'

Prospect and customer experience is all about how you make your interlocutor feel. Doing the proper research, even if it comes out wrong, will be appreciated. When you take someone's time, show some respect by preparing for it. - failing to prepare is preparing to fail- especially when you are in the seller position.

We concluded our talk by addressing the subject of the decision-maker. I wanted to know his thoughts when mine were obvious: the decision-maker *is* this invisible man. There is no such thing as one person making a decision when selling to fortune 500. Thinking about the one decision maker you need to get access to: you cannot get it more wrong.

The Invisible Man : 'There you are! A present from the Invisible Man! Money! Money! Money! Money! Ha-ha-ha!'

'Sellers think that by going high, at the top of the organization, they will sell faster. But then, my CEO looks at me and asks, 'what do you think' and it can go both ways. Even when I want to buy a solution and build a strong case, I have to move things internally. The buying decision process is never about one person. It simply cannot be a one person decision. The process is many people moving multidimensionally. For example, most people leave the procurement behind when they would gain months by involving them from the start. Going to the top is great for those who have done their homework and validate that they have built champions at operational level. Otherwise, you may just look like a fool.'

'You said Champions' I noticed.

Think this is not happening to your organization? Look closer, it is not that....invisible.

The Invisible Man: 'But, these are trivial difficulties. We shall find ways of defeating everything.'

<u>Plot summary</u>

❖ SDRs/BDRs have close to no chance of getting the attention of senior executives unless they have done a hell of a lot of preparation work and used personalisation in their approach.

❖ When Customer Success Managers inherit a situation they hardly know anything about, it reflects on the reputation of the entire company. Worse, when they are not empowered and trained to deal with high level executives it can put the revenue at risk.

❖ Some sellers still cut corners when engaging with prospects, lacking proper preparation before a meeting.

❖ Budget owners are not necessarily economic buyers.. Eg: a CMO may be assigned a budget, but then how he or she will spend it might require the final yes of the Economic Buyer (EB): the person who, if he/she says yes, no one else can say no.

<u>Ready, set, action!</u>

❖ There is no such thing as: have you met the decision makers, so please, sales leader, stop asking that question! Instead, question the mapping of the opportunity and the account, who do we talk to and what are their influences... The budget owner can own a small budget compared to your value. Push the walls, increase your value by listening, understanding your prospect issues and lay out a plan to solve them.

❖ A champion of the do-nothing, a champion of the competition...or the champion of a more critical project might kill your opportunity because he or she is more substantial than yours and make a stronger case to the economic buyer: do not discard them, they could be stronger than yours.

● Don't be scared of having a very high Economic Buyer, challenge your champion on who he/she is..

● If you have a close relationship: most likely a deal champion.

METRICS IN COMPLEX SELLING

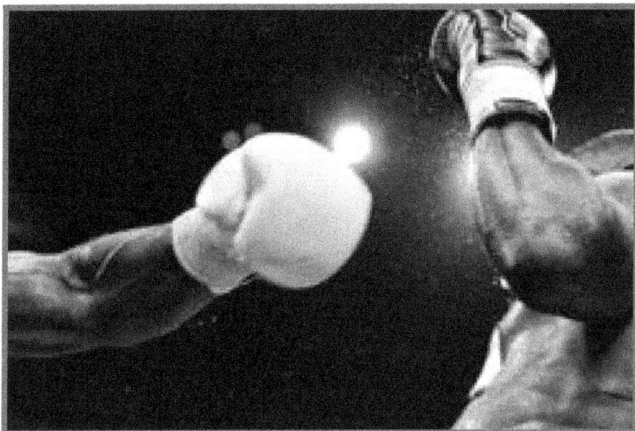

Rocky Balboa

When it comes to running sales in a complex selling environment, measurement and operating rhythm are critical. Much like in boxing, consistency in sales is essential. Many people compare a well oiled sales machine to the military. Personally, I see the military as a little too clean and too organized, that's why I have decided to illustrate how metrics can help you manage, motivate, inspire your revenue teams to success with the iconic Rocky Balboa.

From my perspective, key performance indicators (KPIs) are data that show you just how good you are at attaining your business goals. Meanwhile, metrics track the status of your business processes. There are a number of metrics you can use to take the pulse of your sales team, let's explore a few more to consider:

METRIC #1

Any deal that enters the CRM as a line in the pipeline, should, by default, have **one** touchpoint per week to be a deal. If you cannot build that traction or if you cannot get into that rhythm then it is not a prospect, it is a lead. For each 'forecasted' deal in the quarter, whether that deal sits in upside or commit, the account executive (or sales in charge) must have **three** touch points per week with the prospect/client. Three touchpoints are significant. It means you talk to many people within the organization, multiple champions and coaches, and various departments such as procurement, security and legal. Do not talk to the same person three times a week. That is simple harassment. Failure to be in contact three times a week means that the grasp on the account is limited, that you do not know enough people's account, you have not expanded enough. Without these touchpoints, the risks of not closing on time will increase. For every deal you are working on, remember that you are most likely competing against at least four other suppliers for budget approval, access to legal, security, GDPR, procurement etc; creating a relationship with each of these departments will set you above the pack.

Rocky Balboa: 'Going in one more round when you don't think you can. That's what makes all the difference in your life.'

METRIC #2

For any deal above 100k, you must have at least **two** people with power and influence who have a personal interest in working with you, with your company specifically so that they sell for you when you are not there also called in most methodologies: champions.

You need a person who buys in at the operational level (operational/functional champion) and a person who knows how to justify why the solution will not only solve an operational problem but also its business consequences.

Another metric to consider is that to identify and test your champion you must have talked to at least **five** different people in the organization, otherwise, how do you know he/she has power and influence? Talking to one person who says they have the budget, the power to decide and sign, and that you do not need access to anyone is putting your deal at risk. Expand or you'll never make those **three** touch points a week that are necessary to control your deal to the finish line.

Rocky Balboa: 'I am not the richest, smartest or most talented person in the world, but I succeed because I keep going, and going, and going!'

METRIC #3

Six weeks is the number of weeks that a deal can remain in the pipeline after the beginning of a new quarter.
There are some quarters when it should actually be less; for example in Q3 during summer when no deal goes through if it is not advanced enough in the first month

or in Q4, when everyone wants to wrap their work to finish everything before Christmas.

Running these metrics all year long can enable you to stop operating quarterly. Your company may have obligations to run the business this way, but it does not mean operations should follow. In fact, the more you are going to align with a quarter rhythm, the more damage you may do.

Rocky Balboa: 'Success is usually the culmination of controlling failure.'

Here are a few negative consequences that can occur when you are running your revenue quarterly:

- Sales representative systematically send quotes with validity date aligning with quarter end.
- Sales representatives aligning all their close dates on the last day of the quarter.
- Discounts and conditions given to incentivize closing within the quarter when the customer has not even mentioned the need for it.
- All closing dates and starting dates of contracts are aligned, meaning that all resources are under

pressure to be on board and be delivered all at once.

- Bottleneck around rev ops and legal.
- Forecast accuracy is absolutely messed up.
- Beginning of quarters are slow due to all efforts concentrated on quarter end
- Quarterly Business Reviews are inefficient, indeed, starting to review the deals of the current quarter is already too late.

Some companies think that having calendar asynchronous quarters will help, it can, but it will not solve anything if your reps re-align with the new asynchronous dates.

Duke: 'You're gonna have to go through hell, worse than any nightmare you've ever dreamed. But when it's over, I know you'll be the one standing. You know what you have to do. Do it.'

Instead, run your company like there is no quarter.

<u>Incentivise your entire team to build a pipeline consistently (and weekly) based on the gap.</u>

Build enough pipeline so that you feel comfortable to qualify out deals that are eating your resources and dragging the forecast.

Consistently alig to your prospect's compelling event. A closing date by which the negative business consequences of your prospect's must be solved. (hint: it does not magically match your quarter end)

Educate your prospects on the pains they do not know they have. Being a startup/scale up means you are educating a market: you must create a budget where there is none and urgency when no timeline was planned.

Helping your customer measure the impact of a problem through metrics can therefore be valuable. But, be careful, a conversation about metrics and/or KPIs should not be frustrating for the customers. To uncover metrics in a natural conversational way, dig in when you hear the vague statement such as 'not efficient enough, 'not productive enough,' 'too slow' with the key sentences:

What does this (not efficient, too long, too manual) mean to your organization? (note that this statement for x is not the same for A,B,C clients)

What would be the ideal state (efficient, time, automation) for your organization?

Always try to understand how they determine the statement if they are not measuring it: why is it not enough for your organization?

Last but not least...Be conscious that words like faster, more robust, better, more, increase, improve, etc. are warnings of wishful thinking. When someone wishes to be better, we first need to understand why by uncovering a pain rather than a nice to have. Remember, only a business pain will drive urgency and therefore a reliable close date.

Some deals are meant to close in the first and second month of the quarter because they are in symbiosis with your customer sales cycle. Challenge and align your close plan, resources and negotiation phase to your prospect urgency.

The foundation of a close plan is to have a conversation with your Champion and agree on a go-live date. If you feel uncomfortable having this conversation, you already know something is off. If your champion is pushing back, something is off. Find out what is going on and manage the issues/objections.

At that moment, if anything feels insecure, you must go back to implicating the pains. What are the consequences of leaving things as they are? What are the consequences of not meeting the company's objectives? Can they continue working well without you? That's the compelling event/date you are looking for.

The sooner you know, the sooner you can act on it and change the perspective.

Rocky Balboa: 'Time takes everybody out. Time is undefeated.'

Plot summary

- ❖ Metric #1 : Any deal that enters the CRM should have **one** touchpoint per week to be a deal
- ❖ Metric #2 : For any deal above 100k, you must have at least **two** champions.
- ❖ Metric #3 : **Six** weeks is the number of weeks that a deal can remain in the pipeline after the beginning of a new quarter.

Ready, set, action!

- ❖ How well are you measuring and tracking your activity, the one of your team?
- ❖ How well are you supporting these metrics to be implemented with brainstorming sessions and call to actions?
- ❖ How much do you support qualifying out deals that are leading nowhere?

CLOSING DEALS

Now you see me[30]

Although the following statement applies particularly for the last quarter of the fiscal year, it is critical that the following message be part of your mindset at every moment of closing.

The end of the fiscal year is the quest of the last deals for the vendors, the last budget spent for the buyers, and, in

---

[30] Photo by Julius Drost on Unsplash

the midst of things, the necessity to become a priority, to appear, whether than disappear.

As contracts start signing and others vanish, what other comparison at this time of year than magic. The role of the magician is to make you believe what is true is false and what is wrong is true. This confuses you deeply to the point of making up your own reality. To show you the power of the closing dynamic, I have called upon the four incredibly talented Horsemen from the movie 'Now you see me'.

'Come in close. Closer. Because the more you think you see, the easier it'll be to fool you. You are looking, but what you're really doing is filtering, interpreting teaching for meaning. My job? To take that most precious gift you give me, your attention, and use it against you.'

This is a horseman talking, yet it could be anyone from the procurement department or even the company you are trying to sell to. At the likelihood of signing a contract, most sellers wear their happy ears the minute the buyer admits to a strong interest in buying when they know that this is the first step of a long and complicated adventure.

J. Daniel Atlas: 'Ladies and gentlemen...'
Henley Reeves: 'For our next trick...'
J. Daniel Atlas: 'We are going to rob a bank.'

Selling is not just about getting a purchase order. It is about creating trust and a strong foundation for a long-term customer relationship. The more you think of the close, the less the customer will. As you may have over a thousand reasons to lose a deal, there is only one you shall remember: you haven't explored the unsaid.

J. Daniel Atlas: 'Rule #1 of magic, always be the smartest guy in the room.'

Rule #1 of negotiation, always be the person who has the most information in the room. If you think the discovery is over with your sales stage in the CRM, think about it twice: you're mistaken. Be curious, challenge your customer and ask the question no one else dare asking such as:

What other priorities are you working on? What are the vendors you are engaging with? What else are you doing other than talking with us to fix this issue? (...)

Dylan Rhodes: 'I will be all over you like...'
J. Daniel Atlas:'Llike white on rice.'

Asking smart, open-ended questions shows that you care. But, thinking you are the only vendor your customers are dealing with is self-centered and utopic. You may not compete against a direct competitor. In Q4, it is the period when getting access to the legal department, the procurement department, getting security approval, and access to the ultimate executive for a budget is like entering a roman arena. You are not alone, and everyone wants the same degree of attention. Everyone is competing against you for attention and budget allocation.

What should you do then?

Dylan Rhodes: 'I could care less about magicians in general. What I hate is people who exploit other people.'
Alma Dray: 'Exploit them how?'
Dylan Rhodes: 'By taking advantage of their weaknesses. Their need to believe in something that's unexplainable in order to make their lives more bearable.'

Be their number one priority.

If you cannot be the most significant pain they need to solve, you will be at the bottom of the list.
If you are the most considerable pain they need to solve, you are at the top of their list. It is as simple as that and it is proportional to the allocated budget.

Have you ever been in a position where someone says: all our lawyers are out on vacation? It NEVER happens. What is happening is that all their lawyers are working on a large, enormous, gigantic project and have no time for your budget size.

Arthur Tressler: 'Whatever you stand to make from this, I'll double it.'
Thaddeus Bradley: 'I stand to make $5 million.'
Arthur Tressler: 'Am I flinching.'

If you are solving a significant pain with a rational and emotional impact, the reason to act is vital at a premium. The more you fix, the more attention you will get from all the departments involved in the buying process.

But listen, this is only step one. You need to understand what these departments are going through. Be human, be friendly, care about them as you would care about your champions. Most people only transfer documents between their legal department to their prospect legal department without reading them, understanding them, or challenging them. Be your customer advocate, translate internally what you want to transfer externally.

Be respectful of time, as you are fighting for face time with your customer's department, they will favor the people who are respectful of their time by maximizing efficiency, do not schedule a 60mn meeting if you only need 30, do not ask for a meeting if you can solve it with an email, basic principle.

Conan O'Brien: 'Remember, if the oxygen mask comes down, put it on the lawyer first. Remember.'
Arthur Tressler: 'Oh, yes. I always do. It's the lawyer first, then myself, and then the children.'

There you have it, the simple truth: there are over one thousand reasons to tell you this deal is not going to go through this quarter.

There is only one way you can counter them all : do not overlook the details. Ask the questions that are in your head, to everyone, and repeatedly. Some people call them the 'tough' questions because they are too afraid to ask them:

What happens if we do not do business together before the end of the year? What are the consequences on your business? Who in the organization can say no to this project? Who/what could prevent us from working together? ...

Knowing the truth is always better than assuming or hoping. When you see a situation is going south, you can start crafting a plan to fix it. Hoping is never a strategy.

'When a magician waves his hand and says, 'This is where the magic is happening', the real trick is happening somewhere else. Misdirection.'

Plot summary

- ❖ A verbal agreement is not a signed purchase order
- ❖ Always consider the people who could be more influential than your champions and steal your budget at the last minute
- ❖ Ask the tough questions (the ones you are scared to get an answer to)
- ❖ Never ever overlook the details
- ❖ Protect the time of the people you interact with
- ❖ Protect the time and efficiency of your champion

Ready, set, action!

- ❖ What do you know? What *don't* you know? Ask the questions, do not assume anything.
- ❖ Work with a team, one person alone cannot see all the risks, all the ways a deal can go south, partner with someone you trust to deep dive into the missing pieces.

ABOUT THE AUTHOR

Caroline Franczia (Sprinklr, Datadog) is a seasoned sales expert. After starting her career with large tech companies (Computer Associates, Oracle, BMC Software), she spent four years in the Silicon Valley, soaking in Startup culture.

A regular columnist for Maddyness UK and founder of Uppercut First, she's become, in 2020, the European tech Startups CEO's whisperer through hundreds of office hours.[31] Book yours at https://www.uppercut-first.com/officehours

---

[31] Photo Credit Aurore Vinot www.aurorevinot.com

AUTHOR'S VOICE:

DIVERSITY & INCLUSION

Thelma & Louise

For a long time, I wanted to find the right words. I postponed writing about my own experience because I did not think it was important enough. Boom: that was the first problem. I realize now that it is not about the magnitude of what one has to say, nor the necessity to find the perfect words; the point is to speak and inform.

And to make this a bit lighter and fun of a subject, what better than the raw duo of Thelma and Louise, on a road trip through Mexico to avoid murder charges to support this chapter with their incredible dialogues?

So, the question you may ask is: did I ever suffer from gender inequality?

For a long, long time; I would have told you: 'not at all'. I was trusted and I had a great corporate career, or did I?

Louise Sawyer: 'You get what you settle for.'

Quota or not Quota?

Female or not Female? Diversity is about education. To educate, you must repeat, repeat and repeat again until it is integrated and becomes natural. The debate is not whether positive discrimination and quotas should or should not be, whether we should say female founder, female CEO, female title or just 'the title'. The debate is about changing mentalities at their core, and to do this, any step moving forward is progress.

If Quotas are necessary to set rules for hiring more women, more LGBT, more disabled people, more minorities groups in general, then so be it. Until one day, it will be normal to be a fun, smart, smiling leader or founder without falling into the classic images of female success: the ice queen or the crazy emotional diva.

Louise: 'You've always been crazy, this is just the first chance you've had to express yourself.'

In over fifteen years of career, I have yet to hear a successful sales woman or leader be referred to as an alpha. Why is it commonly accepted to refer to a prosperous man as an Alpha, and why is it that the only translation I have ever heard was 'Diva'. For the record, even the Cambridge dictionary offers the definition of alpha male but does not have its gender equivalent of alpha female.

Max: 'You know, the one thing I can't figure out are these girls real smart or real real lucky?'

Hal Slocumb: 'Don't matter. Brains'll only get you so far and luck always runs out.'

This might just be a silly, pointless reference, except that it's not. While I was finalizing a reasonable, well put argument against a male peer in a leadership meeting, I have been asked publicly and bluntly if I were on my period, by the way, if you wonder, this happened, before the #metoo era.

- For heaven's sake! -

I know for a fact that many women in the tech industry were alleged to have used their charms to close deals or sleep with the boss to get better work conditions. After all, is it so hard to imagine that a woman could combine emotional intelligence, incredible organizational skills and hard working ethic?

Thelma : 'Nobody'd believe us. We'd still get in trouble, we'd still have our lives ruined.'

There is an unsaid, subtle constant reminder that women are either too much or not enough, leaving a print for the most balanced and most accomplished to doubt their right place in a world governed by alpha -male- founders, leaders, investors.

This leads to three typical behavior:

The most common one is the famous **burn out**. By trying to be everything and more, by constantly doubting and working harder to prove, exhaustion takes over. A mental fatigue that cannot be repaired as easily as physical exhaustion. I have personally come close to this situation and witnessed accomplished women going through it.

Louise: 'In the future, when a woman's crying like that, she isn't having any fun!'

Another very common behavior lies in the infamous **Impostor Syndrome**. Despite the tremendous effort from successful women, from the press and diversity actions, many still pass on incredible opportunities because they second guess themselves consistently.

I'm going...I'm not going...Some people don't even hesitate while others are haunted by the Imposter Syndrome.

Many have grown up to believe in beliefs: I needed to attend a prestigious school, I do not have enough diplomas, I have not acquired enough experience.

Thankfully, times change although mentalities evolve slowly.

Another reason for not feeling up to the task is the fear of judgment. Unfortunately, there will always be haters, downgraders, and judgemental characters. Giving our power to the judgement of others, is just giving up on how to lead your life.

When I ever find myself taken by Imposter Syndrome, I remember the remarkable quote from Richard Branson: "If somebody offers you an amazing opportunity but you are not sure you can do it, say yes – then learn how to do it later!"

Louise: 'Think you found your callin?'
Thelma: 'Maybe. Maybe. the call of the wild!'

Last but not least, in recent years, I have learned that happiness might be elsewhere: where your work finally meets your personal conviction. I have been approached by my direct and indirect network on how to make such a move. Working for Uppercut First has been a fantastic journey. Choosing my clients working alongside CEOs and executives, learning with them and from them, I have grown to be exactly where I wanted to be. Not 'just' a sales expert, not 'just' a manager, not 'just' a coach: someone who can think, who can solve puzzles, and come up with processes that will have an impact - not 'just' on the sales side but the entire revenue stream and process of the company. Someone who can talk to CPOs and CTOs and bring value to the table and I am finally at peace with owning this title.

Thelma: 'I feel really awake. I don't recall ever feeling this awake. You know? Everything looks different now. You feel like that? You feel like you got something to live for now?'

How can you change things? (tip of the iceberg...)

If you are doubtful about the gender situation, there is one thing that cannot be denied, according to the World Economic Forum's Global Gender Gap Report 2023[32], the global gender gap has increased by a generation from 99.5 years to 135.6 years

---

[32]https://app.50intech.com/discuss/global-gender-gap-report-2021-how-was-your-life-affected-this-year?ngsw-bypass=&utm_source=weekly&utm_medium=email&utm_campaign=weekly-21-04-07

You may be doing the right thing already. But, are your colleagues, executives, co-workers aligned with your values? Don't overlook the white boys club. Ask yourself: are you actively changing things or passively approving the change?

Louise : 'Yeah, where do you get off behaving like that with women you don't even know? Huh? Huh? How'd you feel if someone did that to your mother? Or your sister? Or your wife?'

Advice to women: own your worth, own your happiness and speak up. Do not try to just fit in. Be a woman who empowers women. Be proud.

Advice to the boardroom: how diverse are the boards you attend/hold? You have a play in this. Do the right thing. This is the year of 2023 and female founders are still struggling to be credible and gain founding.

TO CONTINUE

MEDDICC, Andy Whyte

The Qualified Sales Leader, John McMahon

Getting things done, David Allen

KPI checklist, Bernie Smith

Learning to Scale, Regis Medina

First, break all the rules, Gallup

Radical Focus, Christina Wodtke

Measure What Matters, John Doerr

High Output Management, Andrew Grove

The hard thing about hard things, Ben Horowitz

Crossing the Chasm, Geoffrey Moore

THANK YOU

This part makes me nervous because no matter how much care I put into this, I will forget essential people.

Or, as Dori (in Nemo) would say in Nemo 'I don't want to forget'.

A crew of people lifted this book to the finish line; without them, it would still not be out by now.

Veronica Prato Pereira, an Extraordinary Graphic Designer, had the cover finished before I had a table of content ready.

Morgan Perry, for giving me the idea of a book in the first place and promoting Popcorn one.

Celia Goletto, master in kicking my butt at the right time.

Eleanor Manley, for being incredibly engaged and thorough as an Alpha reader.

Jenny Herald, for co-writing the OKR chapter and being an Alpha reader.

David Keribin, for signing up to be a Beta reader when I just had the idea for book 2 and for his unconditional support and feedback in getting it done.

Jennifer Timerman, positive and encouraging critics to anchor the concepts even more. I am happy you could fit this Beta reading into your agenda.

David Johnson - though he's been a bit too kind on deadlines- for always being the Pop culture and business partner editor one can dream of.

Romain Vidal and Jerome Joaug, the out-of-ordinary VCs, for their kindness and sharpness in delivering blunt honesty and powerful feedback that changed the face of the manuscript.

Andy Whyte, you are a true partner my friend, thank you for your support along the years and for accepting to kick off this book!

Jen Allen, I have been a fan of your Winning the Challenger sales podcast from day one. Your LinkedIn posts enlighten my day with witty, fun, and wise words. It is an honor to have you in the foreword of this book. I am thrilled to watch what you are doing with Lavender.ai!

The 117 people who responded 'interested' to the 'would you like to be a Beta reader?' newsletter.

'You guys made me ink.' -Pearl in Nemo

To the many podcast hosts who have interviewed me in the last two years and helped spread the word on snackable, digestible content and Popcorn in business.

For our regular talks, David Khan, Ivan Smets, Seb Boitelle, Romaric Philogène, and Gary Roth make me feel like we could be colleagues.

To the incredibly talented women surrounding me, Caro, Carine, Barbara, Florence, Cécile, Virginie, Océane, Anne-So, and all the many more I cannot list.

Last but not least, the BMC crew (they know who), the Sprinklr crew (no need for names), the Datadog and Confluent crews...and the inspiring managers, leaders, and mentors I still have lunch, dinner, and regular talks with.

And, of course, to my entire family, parents, husband, and kiddos for their unconditional support.

'I forget things almost instantly. It runs in my family... well, at least I think it does... hmm, where are they?'
-Dory